Current
CONTROVERSIES

Issues in Adoption

Other Books in the Current Controversies Series

Aid to Africa

Alternative Therapies

Anger Management

The Arms Trade

Assisted Suicide

Biodiversity

Blogs

Carbon Offsets

Disaster Response

Domestic Wiretapping

Family Violence

Global Warming

Guns and Violence

Homeland Security

Homeschooling

Importing from China

Media Ethics

Prescription Drugs

Rap Music and Culture

The Rights of Animals

Torture

Urban Sprawl

Vaccines

The Wage Gap

Issues in Adoption

Christina Fisanick

GREENHAVEN PRESS
A part of Gale, Cengage Learning

GALE
CENGAGE Learning™

Detroit • New York • San Francisco • New Haven, Conn • Waterville, Maine • London

GALE
CENGAGE Learning™

Christine Nasso, *Publisher*
Elizabeth Des Chenes, *Managing Editor*

© 2009 Greenhaven Press, a part of Gale, Cengage Learning

Gale and Greenhaven Press are registered trademarks used herein under license.

For more information, contact:
Greenhaven Press
27500 Drake Rd.
Farmington Hills, MI 48331-3535
Or you can visit our Internet site at gale.cengage.com

For product information and technology assistance, contact us at

Gale Customer Support, 1-800-877-4253
For permission to use material from this text or product, submit all requests online at www.cengage.com/permissions

Further permissions questions can be emailed to permissionrequest@cengage.com

Articles in Greenhaven Press anthologies are often edited for length to meet page require-ments. In addition, original titles of these works are changed to clearly present the main thesis and to explicitly indicate the author's opinion. Every effort is made to ensure that Greenhaven Press accurately reflects the original intent of the authors. Every effort has been made to trace the owners of copyrighted material.

Cover image reproduced from Ullamaija Hanninen/Gorilla Creative Images/Getty Images.

LIBRARY OF CONGRESS CATALOGING-IN-PUBLICATION DATA

Issues in Adoption / Christina Fisanick, book editor.
    p. cm. -- (Current controversies)
  Includes bibliographical references and index.
  ISBN 978-0-7377-4324-1 (hardcover)
  ISBN 978-0-7377-4323-4 (pbk.)
  1. Adoption--United States. I. Fisanick, Christina.
  HV875.55.I867 2009
  362.7340973--dc22

                                        2009012036

Printed in Mexico
2 3 4 5 6 7 13 12 11 10

Contents

Foreword   11

Introduction   14

Chapter 1: Do Adoptions Need More Regulation?

Chapter Preface   18

Yes: Adoptions Need More Regulation

Laws Regarding Birth Fathers Are   20
Not Clearly Stated or Followed
  Wendy McElroy

  A recent New Mexico adoption case reveals the inherent
  flaws in the current system in regard to fathers' rights. To
  avoid confusion, fathers should be contacted before the
  child is put up for adoption.

Lack of International Adoption Regulation   24
Can Lead to Uncertainties and Corruption
  Kit R. Roane

  Due to a lack of regulation and an inability to enforce
  U.S. adoption laws, international adoptions are often
  fraught with unseen complications and heartbreak.

Lack of Regulation Allows Children to   31
Be Unwillingly Put Up for Adoption
  Russell Goldman

  Despite recent regulations, international adoptions are
  still fraught with deception, including children being put
  up for adoption who have been taken unfairly from their
  birth parents.

More Adoption Regulations Are   38
Needed to Prevent Potential Parents
from Being Deceived
  Michael Crowley

  Although failed international adoptions often receive the
  most publicity, domestic adoptions fail just as frequently
  and are equally devastating; therefore, more regulations
  are necessary to prevent fraudulence and heartache.

**No: Adoptions Do Not Need
More Regulation**

America's Adoption System Is Effective
Because It Is Not Overregulated
Caitriona Palmer

42

Shorter waiting lists, lower costs, and fewer regulations
make U.S. children a good choice for adoptive parents
from the United Kingdom.

China's New Adoption Regulations
Will Prevent Many Americans from
Adopting Children
Elisa Poncz

47

China's new, stricter adoption guidelines will prevent
many U.S. citizens, especially single people and homosexual couples, from adopting children.

Implementation of the Hague Convention
Will Harm American Adoption Agencies
and Potential Parents
Denise L. Behreandt

56

Although the Hague Convention on Intercountry Adoption is meant to make adoptions more ethical, in reality
the stricter regulations will force some adoption agencies
out of business, and many couples will remain childless.

Chapter 2: What Risks and Benefits May Accompany International Adoptions?

Chapter Preface

62

International Adoptions Should Adhere
to the Hague Convention
The United Nations Children's Fund

64

Due to potential corruption, lack of sufficient regulation,
and the best interests of children, international adoptions
should be considered only when other options have been
exhausted.

International Adoption Can Benefit   67
Older Potential Parents
    Marie Pruden

    Older couples attempting to adopt may benefit from
    seeking adoptees abroad.

International Adoption Can Be a Viable   74
Option for African Orphans
    Jini L. Roby and Stacey A. Shaw

    International adoption can be one of many possible solu-
    tions to the African orphan crisis caused by AIDS and
    civil wars, but it should be sought only as a last resort.

Adopting Children from China Can   84
Be Fraught with Corruption
    Anita M. Andrew

    Lack of regulation and oversight of adoptions from China
    has led to a flourishing black market that puts children
    and potential parents at risk.

Chapter 3: Should Adoptive and Birth Families Be Allowed Contact with Each Other?

Chapter Preface   94

Yes: Adoptive and Birth Families Should Be Allowed Contact

Open Adoption Leads to Closeness   96
Between Both Families
    Michael Winerip

    All parties involved in an adoption can benefit from de-
    veloping relationships through the open adoption pro-
    cess.

Closed Adoption Can Sow Bitterness   101
and Discontent
    Marcy Axness

    Truly open adoptions eliminate much of the anguish that
    goes along with so many adoptions.

**No: Adoptive and Birth Families
Should Not Be Allowed Contact**

Privacy in Adoption Is a Human Right   **111**

   Thomas C. Atwood

    It is essential that birth parents who choose confidential
    adoptions have their rights honored.

Open Adoption Can Lead to Heartache   **122**
for Both Families

   Sonia Nazario

    Some open adoptions can harm children and their
    adopted families because of insecurities on the part of
    birth parents and adoptees.

Chapter 4: What Issues Are Involved in Nontraditional Adoptions?

Chapter Preface   **134**

Adoption by Gay Men and Lesbians Is a   **136**
Good Option for Orphaned Children

   Julian Sanchez

    Given the large number of orphaned children in the
    United States, gays and lesbians should be permitted to
    adopt. Not only will it benefit the children, but it is also
    a civil right.

Gay Men and Lesbians Should Not   **146**
Be Allowed to Adopt Children

   Glenn T. Stanton

    Evidence clearly shows that adoption by same-sex couples
    is detrimental to children.

Transgendered Persons Should Be Permitted   **155**
to Have Custody of Children

   Kari Carter

    No studies show that transgendered persons cannot be
    effective parents; therefore, they should be given the op-
    portunity to do what is in the best interests of the child.

Adoption or Long-Term Placement with   165
Relatives Is Better than Foster Care
  Mark Testa, Nancy Sidote Salyers, Mike Shaver,
  and Jennifer Miller
  The U.S. government should assist relatives with providing homes for children in need. Children who live with
  relatives fair better than children in the traditional foster
  care system.

Grandmothers Who Raise Their   173
Grandchildren Experience More Stress
  Terry L. Mills, Zenata Gomez-Smith, and Jessica
  M. De Leon
  Grandparents, specifically young grandmothers, raising
  their grandchildren are under enormous physical, psy-
  chological, and financial burdens.

Organizations to Contact   182

Bibliography   189

Index   194

Foreword

By definition, controversies are "discussions of questions in which opposing opinions clash" (Webster's Twentieth Century Dictionary Unabridged). Few would deny that controversies are a pervasive part of the human condition and exist on virtually every level of human enterprise. Controversies transpire between individuals and among groups, within nations and between nations. Controversies supply the grist necessary for progress by providing challenges and challengers to the status quo. They also create atmospheres where strife and warfare can flourish. A world without controversies would be a peaceful world; but it also would be, by and large, static and prosaic.

The Series' Purpose

The purpose of the Current Controversies series is to explore many of the social, political, and economic controversies dominating the national and international scenes today. Titles selected for inclusion in the series are highly focused and specific. For example, from the larger category of criminal justice, Current Controversies deals with specific topics such as police brutality, gun control, white collar crime, and others. The debates in Current Controversies also are presented in a useful, timeless fashion. Articles and book excerpts included in each title are selected if they contribute valuable, long-range ideas to the overall debate. And wherever possible, current information is enhanced with historical documents and other relevant materials. Thus, while individual titles are current in focus, every effort is made to ensure that they will not become quickly outdated. Books in the Current Controversies series will remain important resources for librarians, teachers, and students for many years.

In addition to keeping the titles focused and specific, great care is taken in the editorial format of each book in the series. Book introductions and chapter prefaces are offered to provide background material for readers. Chapters are organized around several key questions that are answered with diverse opinions representing all points on the political spectrum. Materials in each chapter include opinions in which authors clearly disagree as well as alternative opinions in which authors may agree on a broader issue but disagree on the possible solutions. In this way, the content of each volume in Current Controversies mirrors the mosaic of opinions encountered in society. Readers will quickly realize that there are many viable answers to these complex issues. By questioning each author's conclusions, students and casual readers can begin to develop the critical thinking skills so important to evaluating opinionated material.

Current Controversies is also ideal for controlled research. Each anthology in the series is composed of primary sources taken from a wide gamut of informational categories including periodicals, newspapers, books, U.S. and foreign government documents, and the publications of private and public organizations. Readers will find factual support for reports, debates, and research papers covering all areas of important issues. In addition, an annotated table of contents, an index, a book and periodical bibliography, and a list of organizations to contact are included in each book to expedite further research.

Perhaps more than ever before in history, people are confronted with diverse and contradictory information. During the Persian Gulf War, for example, the public was not only treated to minute-to-minute coverage of the war, it was also inundated with critiques of the coverage and countless analyses of the factors motivating U.S. involvement. Being able to sort through the plethora of opinions accompanying today's major issues, and to draw one's own conclusions, can be a complicated and frustrating struggle. It is the editors' hope that Current Controversies will help readers with this struggle.

Introduction

"*Whether celebrity adoptions have created a trend for international adoption remains to be seen.*"

Recent headlines have put international adoptions in the spotlight following a rise in celebrity adoptions from other countries. Stars such as Madonna, Angelina Jolie, and Meg Ryan have adopted children from Ethiopia, Malawi, Cambodia, and China. U.S. State Department records show that each year more than 25,000 children are adopted from countries around the world with China, Russia, and Guatemala regularly topping the list. The profiling of celebrity adoptions might encourage others to adopt orphaned children from around the world; however, the apparent ease with which these celebrities adopt can be misleading for most Americans who do not have access to unlimited resources or the advantage of worldwide fame.

Widespread interest in adopting children from other nations began less than a hundred years ago. The first wave of international adoptions occurred shortly after World War I left many children without parents. Other wars prompted countries to make their children available for adoption, including Korea and Vietnam. In other cases, extreme poverty and overpopulation encouraged nations such as Russia and China to allow foreigners to adopt. Most recently, the AIDS crisis has prompted African nations to open their borders to potential parents. Melissa Fay Greene, author of *There Is No Me Without You*, argues this trend will increase as AIDS claims more and more lives in the next decade. Given these dire global situations, it is no wonder international leaders encourage people from more prosperous lands to adopt their orphaned children.

On the other hand, the potential for the world's wealthiest citizens, such as celebrities, to exploit birth parents and children from impoverished nations can be quite high. Harvard University Law professor Elizabeth Bartholet expresses her concern about these potential dangers. She notes, "many see international adoption as one of the ultimate forms of human exploitation, with the rich, powerful, and white taking from poor, powerless members of racial and other minority groups their children, thus imposing on those who have little what many of us might think of as the ultimate loss." Although she is quick to argue that international adoption might be the only way to help some of these children, she cautions that "we must address the problems of poverty and injustice that result in children being abandoned in large numbers in the poor countries of the world."

Most media coverage makes Americans believe that international adoptions are simple. In reality they can take many years to complete, and some are never successful. In fact, following China's changes to their adoption policies in 2006, hundreds of waiting couples were notified that their adoptions had been cancelled. Other potential parents may think adopting children from other lands is glamorous and are not prepared for the reality of raising children from other cultures. Christina Crawford, adopted daughter of late actress Joan Crawford, has spoken out against high-profile celebrity adoptions. *Mommy Dearest*, her best-selling book that was later made into a movie, chronicles her claims of an extremely abusive childhood. She later discovered that her birth parents were alive when she was adopted, despite what she was told by her adoptive mother. In an article in *The Observer*, she comments on adoptions by Madonna and other stars: "From the adoptee's point of view, it is vitally important to know who they are, where they came from, or it can have profound medical and psychological effects."

Still, some adoption advocates claim celebrities who adopt have been unfairly targeted by reporters who do not understand the hurdles they must go through to bring their children home. According to a recent article in *People* magazine, "Interviews with dozens of adoption agency officials, attorneys who specialize in private adoption, and adoptive celebrities themselves reveal a far different scenario—one in which the stars, like other adoptive parents, undergo intense scrutiny and often endure long waits and disappointment before realizing their dream." Therefore, it appears the only advantage celebrities have over others is money, and even that has its limitations. David Radis, a Los Angeles attorney who has worked with many celebrities on adoption cases, says that "it's a myth" that celebrity adoptions are easier. "They have just as many problems, if not more, adopting."

As restrictions on global adoptions increase in response to claims of exploitation and abuse, potential parents will find it even harder to bring home a child of their own. Whether celebrity adoptions have created a trend for international adoption remains to be seen. The authors in *Current Controversies: Issues in Adoption* debate current views on adoption in the following chapters: Do Adoptions Need More Regulation?, Should International Adoptions Be Encouraged?, Should Adoptive and Birth Families Be Allowed Contact?, and What Issues Are Involved in Nontraditional Adoptions? In the end, most people would agree that encouraging the safe, legal adoption of orphaned children can only help make the world a better place.

CHAPTER 1

Do Adoptions Need More Regulation?

Chapter Preface

In the past decade, major changes have taken place in adoption processes around the world. The Hague Convention on Protection of Children and Co-operation in Respect of Intercountry Adoption, which went into effect in the United States on April 1, 2008, is the most pervasive of those changes and works to protect children and their birth and adoptive parents from deception and other abuses. Although few people would object to protecting the safety of other humans, especially children, some have found country-specific adoption conditions to be unfair and unreasonable.

The need for the Hague Convention on Adoption arose out of concerns that children were being abducted and sold into adoption. In addition, adoptive parents were being taken advantage of because there were few regulations protecting their rights: Birth parents or adoption agencies would enter into adoption agreements without ever intending to surrender the child to the adoptive parents. The main stipulation of the convention that one central agency in each country be in charge of all international adoptions is intended to ensure the safety and security of all parties involved. According to the U.S. Citizenship and Immigration Services, "It ultimately provides a framework for member countries to work together to ensure that children are provided with permanent, loving homes, that adoptions take place in the best interests of a child, and that the abduction, sale, or trafficking in children is prevented."

In addition to ratifying the Hague Convention on Adoption, some of the seventy-five member countries have recently added other adoption regulations. Some potential parents have found fault with these restrictions, noting that successful adoptions were already difficult. In 2006, China released a new set of adoption guidelines that drew the attention of the international media. Along with rules in regard to age, income, and marital status, people adopting children from China must have a body mass index lower than 40, which according to global health measurements indicates chronic, morbid obesity. In response to the weight requirement, Dr. David Katz of the Yale University School of Medicine argues that there is no scientific proof demonstrating that obese people do not make good parents. He further notes that "singling out obesity as a measure of health just because it happens to be detectable is neither rational, nor fair."

Clearly, regulations are needed to provide stability and safety to all parties involved, but some people worry that restrictions based on superficial characteristics only add to the already difficult adoption process. In the end, both sides of the debate want what is in the best interests of children. How best to determine and enforce those interests are explored in the viewpoints of the following chapter.

Laws Regarding Birth Fathers Are Not Clearly Stated or Followed

Wendy McElroy

Wendy McElroy is the author of numerous books, including XXX: A Woman's Right to Pornography. *She also is a regular contributor to www.ifeminists.com, an online organization that supports feminists who seek individual responsibility for their lives.*

On July 26, [2006,] the New Mexico Court of Appeals reversed a lower court decision that terminated the parental rights of a biological father. The precedent-setting case concerns 'a deadbolt dad'—that is, a father locked out of his child's life, in this case by adoption.

At three days old, Mark Huddleston's son was placed with a family who eventually adopted him. Huddleston learned of his son when the baby was two months old; he immediately pursued custody. The ensuing legal battle took two years and the child is now 2-1/2. He may soon be ripped from the only parents he has known and given to a stranger.

But, if that stranger is a loving biological dad, then doesn't the father have a right to raise his own son?

The dilemma was created by an adoption agency that acted with no regard for the biological bonds that constitute family. In doing so, it expressed society's general dismissal of a biological father's role in adoption. In turn, a district court treated that role with less respect than is customarily accorded to a mother's.

The question of whom the child calls 'daddy' will almost certainly go to the state's Supreme Court. As a result, a young

Wendy McElroy, "Adoption, Fathers' Rights Tangle Threatens Child," www .iFeminists.com, August 8, 2006. Reproduced by permission.

boy may be psychologically damaged forever. Moreover, a chill may fall over adoptions in New Mexico as potential parents watch their worst fear unfold in court: a biological parent demands custody of a legally adopted child.

The pain and pathos were unnecessary.

Case Details

The details of this case are as follows.

In 2003, the then-divorced Huddleston broke up on bad terms with a woman who gave birth eight months later. Huddleston, who is also the father of two grown children, said he did not know of the pregnancy.

On April 23, 2004, the re-married Huddleston received a letter from the private agency Adoptions Plus. It alerted him to his possible paternity of a child who had been placed for adoption two months prior.

The next morning, the Huddlestons met with the executive director of Adoptions Plus. She said the agency had known of his possible paternity before the child's birth and had attempted to contact him. At this point, however, they said he no longer had rights to be asserted.

On April 27, Huddleston filed a lawsuit to gain custody; resulting DNA tests proved his paternity.

At the same time and at Huddleston's request, the New Mexico Children, Youth and Families Department (CYFD) investigated Adoptions Plus, for whom CYFD is the controlling authority. CYFD found the agency had not made diligent efforts to contact Huddleston and ordered the baby returned to one of its biological parents.

Before the order was enforced, however, the case went to trial with the court permitting supervised visitation to Huddleston. On Jan. 5, 2005, he saw his 11-month-old son for the first time.

On March 10, the court terminated Huddleston's parental rights.

The judge's decision was based on two factors: he believed the mother when she said Huddleston knew of the pregnancy; and, the child had bonded with adoptive parents Bobby and Rosario Romero.

Whether he knew of the pregnancy, his consent was still required for the adoption.

They finalized the adoption despite Huddleston's clear intent to appeal.

He succeeded. On July 26, the Appeals Court found the lower court had "improperly focused on Mark's pre-birth conduct, and thus the court's finding that Mark presumptively abandoned the child is not supported by substantial evidence."

In short, whether he knew of the pregnancy, his consent was still required for the adoption. The judge may have agreed with Huddleston's argument that spending over two years and $60,000 in pursuing custody was evidence of *non-*abandonment.

The Court also found that New Mexico law does not close the door on last-minute claims, thus allowing biological fathers to contest an adoption up to the moment it is finalized.

The case has been thrown back to the lower court but it is unlikely to end there. The Rosarios are determined to appeal an unfavorable ruling to the state Supreme Court. For his part, Huddleston is currently filing for immediate visitation rights and ultimate custody. Meanwhile, the child remains with the Romeros; Huddleston has not seen his son in a year.

A Possible Solution

How can another such nightmare be prevented in New Mexico and elsewhere?

As a solution, some point to putative (or alleged) father registries, which differ from state-to-state. In effect, the registries say that a man who has unprotected sex with a woman must report it to the state within varying time limits surrounding a child's birth in order to retain his parental rights in adoption. (Huddleston registered in New Mexico after discovering his paternity.)

Others argue that having to register one-night stands in state registries in order to preserve parental rights places an unequal burden upon the father. After all, if a child results, the man is almost automatically held responsible for child support. Why are his rights less automatic than his responsibilities?

Instead, why not simply seek disclosure of all potential fathers and due diligence in contacting them?

Michael McCormick of the [Washington,] D.C.-based American Coalition for Fathers and Children believes the problem is anti-father bias in the family court. He believes Huddleston is the victim of an adoption agency that saw fathers "as a hindrance."

Whatever solution is implemented, it is not likely to guarantee that another Huddleston-style tragedy will not occur; sometimes biological fathers cannot be found. But taking a father's rights and consent as seriously as a mother's would vastly reduce the incidence.

Meanwhile, people who wonder why 'foreign' adoptions are so popular need look no farther than Huddleston. Adopting a child from China may be a bureaucratic maze, but it eliminates the prospect of a biological parent showing up on the doorstep.

Lack of International Adoption Regulation Can Lead to Uncertainties and Corruption

Kit R. Roane

Kit R. Roane is a journalist, screenwriter, and photographer. His work has appeared in various media outlets, and for several years he served as a senior writer for U.S. News and World Report, *in which the following viewpoint appeared.*

All Carrie West wanted was a chance to care for an orphaned child. But when she traveled to Vietnam five years ago, she says, she got something else: a quick lesson on the murky world of international adoptions. Here's how she tells the story: Informed by her adoption facilitator that Thuy, the little girl she had planned to adopt, had fallen deathly ill with tuberculosis, she ended up taking a different child. But Thuy's plight stayed with her, and she sought out updates on her condition. Eventually, she learned that the child, far from being ill or convalescing, had been adopted by someone else— long before.

With no official government agency to handle the incident, West took her story to the Internet, writing on adoption blogs and other websites about the facilitator she says did her wrong. The facilitator, Mai-Ly Latrace, responded with a libel lawsuit, which so far names three couples, including West and her husband.

The suit, filed last year, highlighted some of what can go wrong in the fast-growing world of international adoptions. Last year, there were nearly 23,000 adoptions from overseas by

American parents, a number that has been increasing as domestic adoptions become more rare. "Your neighborhood health club is more heavily regulated," says Trish Maskew, executive director of Ethica, a nonprofit outfit that advocates for better international adoption laws. "The industry allows unlicensed facilitators to work without oversight. The U.S. government refuses to act, and consumers walk into this blind."

The libel lawsuit filed by Latrace is based on some contentious issues. Latrace asserts that she has been unjustly maligned by West and the other defendants in the case who criticized her role in facilitating adoptions for them. The critics, on the other hand, point to, among other things, a letter from the Embassy of Vietnam in Washington from March 2005 stating that Latrace is "a child trafficker for money." She was deported from Vietnam, the letter says, on Oct. 18, 2002. The embassy's press attaché, Chien Bach, confirmed the authenticity of the letter and added that Latrace "is banned from entering" Vietnam. Latrace says she knows nothing about any of this, saying that she encountered problems with Vietnamese immigration authorities who revoked her visa when she used the wrong type on a trip to the country. But, she says, she traveled to Vietnam just last year and encountered no legal troubles there. Latrace's attorney says that the embassy's letter about Latrace's alleged child-trafficking activities is based on inaccurate and unsubstantiated information.

Latrace proudly defends her work, saying she has helped hundreds of people adopt children overseas and that she filed her lawsuit only after critics forced her hand by falsely accusing her of improper and unethical conduct. Any bad experiences would-be adoptive parents may have had, she says, were the result of miscommunication. She adds that some difficulties were the fault of her mother, Marie Latrace, with whom she has worked in the past, including West's adoption. (Marie Latrace, who lives with her daughter denies that she did anything wrong while facilitating adoptions.) Latrace says that the defendants in her lawsuit, along with U.S. immigration agents in Vietnam, have long been out to get her. She also says that she has an affidavit from a Vietnamese couple that shows that they gave up their child willingly. "I never sold a child. I have never bought a child," Latrace told *U.S. News*. "And I don't know why anyone in Vietnam is saying that I was involved in anything that was criminal. Especially when it comes to kids." Latrace is seeking monetary damages, as well as expenses, interest, and attorney's fees.

Adopting a child from overseas is anything but simple.

The dispute with West and the other defendants in the lawsuit is not the only source of contention involving Latrace. In 1995, a South Carolina adoption agency filed a criminal complaint against her. The local police department incident report says that the owner of the adoption agency accused Latrace of hoarding "clothes, shoes, medicine, etc." that were supposed to have been delivered to an orphanage in Vietnam. A judge ordered Latrace to complete 40 hours of community service; she did so, and the charges against her were dropped. Latrace blames the incident on a custody dispute with her husband, and says she always intended to deliver the items to Vietnam.

There were other issues as well, and like many in the often-confusing world of international adoptions, they are tangled. Tedi Hedstrom, the owner of Tedi Bear Adoptions, worked with Latrace during the period in which West was attempting to adopt. Hedstrom voluntarily relinquished her license to Florida authorities in March 2003 after the state found several violations, including having personnel files that lacked proof that workers had been screened or met training requirements. But Hedstrom, who now works in Georgia, blames Latrace. "My agency had only one registered complaint in seven years; we had an excellent reputation," she says. "After I began working with Mai-Ly, we had approximately 30 complaints all directly related to her within a very short period, a couple of months. I believe that choosing to work with Mai-Ly Latrace was the worst business decision I have ever made in my entire life." Latrace says Hedstrom caused her own difficulties and points out that the state's complaint never mentions her.

Adopting a child from overseas is anything but simple. Federal agents who investigated a Seattle adoption agency run by two sisters, for instance, documented evidence of visa fraud and money laundering. The agents spent more than two years tracking international money flows and searching Cambodia for witnesses and found that children were being bought from their Cambodian parents and brought to the United States with fraudulent identification documents. Some Cambodians thought they were sending their children to an orphanage school and could always pick them up. "There were huge amounts of money being made, being promised to orphanages in Cambodia, that was instead being diverted for bribes and for luxury items," says Michael Barr, the lead prosecutor. In the course of the investigation, agents found that "facilitators would line up several different groups of parents for a child," says Bill Strassberger, a spokesman for the Department of Homeland Security, which now handles immigration crimes.

Happy Clients

In the Florida lawsuit, West says, she spoke out because of similar issues. She says she stuck her neck out "and sometimes you get it cut off. I'm paying tens of thousands of dollars to say what is true." Thuy, the child she had initially been set to adopt, is living today in Saipan with Judi Mosley who is also named in Latrace's lawsuit. West says that several months after Thuy had been adopted by Mosley, Latrace wrote West, stating that Thuy and her sister were now living with a social worker and that "Thuy is still receiving medical care." Latrace maintains that she conducted her relationship with West properly and that she relied on a Vietnamese social worker for the information she conveyed to West.

In 2002, West says, Latrace began soliciting funds to build an orphanage in Thuy's name. It was only a few months before this time, West says, that she found out that Thuy wasn't ill and had already been adopted by Mosley. West and Mosley then contacted Latrace to arrange another adoption for Mosley. Latrace, West says, offered Thuy. Latrace says that the Vietnamese social worker lied to her about Thuy's status and blames that for the mix-up.

Adoption agencies, and the facilitators they work with, can sometimes leave would-be adoptive parents in agonizing dilemmas.

Latrace has many happy and satisfied clients, she says, among them Bruce and Debbie Hofman in Florida, who used Latrace to facilitate the adoption of three babies and a toddler in Vietnam. "Mai-Ly made things happen that wouldn't have happened," Debbie Hofman says, adding that Latrace successfully shepherded them through a very complicated process.

Requirements

Whatever the outcome of the dispute, it appears to show how adoption agencies, and the facilitators they work with, can sometimes leave would-be adoptive parents in agonizing dilemmas. With so few rules and regulations, many have nowhere to turn. In Florida, full-time employees of adoption agencies must pass background checks and meet minimum degree and experience requirements. But that does not apply to those who call themselves "consultants," such as Latrace, who says that her only qualification is on-the-job training. Following calls by *U.S. News*, the Florida Department of Children and Families did an unannounced check of Little Pearls, the adoption agency Latrace has been working with in Tampa. Andy Ritter, a DCF spokesman, says investigators found evidence suggesting that Latrace should be deemed an employee of the agency for regulatory purposes, such as her use of a company cellphone. They also found that Latrace was telling prospective clients that she was Little Pearl's facilitator for Guatemalan adoptions and soliciting fees "in excess of $25,000" that could be paid either to Little Pearls or to her own consulting firm, HQ Online.

The DCF also found some licensing violations at Little Pearls, including evidence of employees working in the agency who had not been screened and approved by the department. Ritter said that the agency's paperwork was not in order, among other problems. Asked about further documentation, Ritter provided a follow-up letter stating that the agency's owner, a bankruptcy attorney named Richard Feinberg, told DCF investigators as far back as June 2004 that Latrace "was not involved as an employee or as an independent contractor facilitating or assisting in adoptions" and that her only work for Feinberg had consisted in her designing the website for another adoption agency he sought to license. "You stated that the website design was her only activity . . . and that she no longer had, nor would she have, any relationship with your practice and Little Pearls," the letter says.

But Feinberg told *U.S. News* that Latrace has worked directly with clients, answered their E-mails, and generally helped facilitate adoptions. Feinberg added that Latrace does an "excellent job" and is "the most devoted and dedicated adoption advocate" he has ever met. Feinberg says that he is currently restructuring the business and that the agency is not taking on any new adoptions at this time.

Ritter acknowledges that the state's power over adoption facilitators is very limited. Even if the state had done a background check on Latrace, "problems in another country probably would not come back," says Ritter. He adds that Latrace's consulting firm is not licensed to do adoptions in Florida. But the state is powerless if she continues to work with clients outside the state, Ritter says.

In other words, *caveat* adopter. Advocates are hopeful that the Hague Convention on International Adoption, signed by President Bill Clinton in 2000 but yet to be ratified, will provide greater oversight and transparency of at least some international adoptions if it is correctly implemented; some experts have their doubts. For one thing, says Maskew, it will apply only when both countries involved in an adoption have ratified it. And the hottest countries for foreign adoptions haven't. Still, it has to be better than the options parents have now: scouring the Internet or trying to pry useful information out of state regulators. Maskew says that facilitators and agencies have been known to post glowing referrals about themselves online under fake screen names. She adds that some also try to curtail complaints by making prospective clients sign blank confidentiality agreements and liability waivers. The states have been no more helpful: According to a 2004 Ethica report, when would-be parents "do manage to reach a licensing specialist, they are often told that the state does not keep complaints on file or that they cannot be released to the public." More often still, Ethica says, regulators just don't answer the phone.

Lack of Regulation Allows Children to Be Unwillingly Put Up for Adoption

Russell Goldman

Russell Goldman is a regular contributor to ABCNEWS.com and its subsidiaries.

Moments after their newly adopted adolescent daughters stepped off the plane from India in 1998, Desiree and David Smolin knew something was wrong.

"The agency told us the girls were eager to be adopted and eager to come to the U.S.," Desiree Smolin told ABCNEWS-.com. "But in reality, the girls were in terrible, terrible emotional shape. They were avoidant and deeply depressed; one of them was suicidal. I had never seen people so emotionally disturbed in my entire life."

It took weeks before the couple learned the reason for the girls' distress.

Manjula and Bhagya told their adoptive parents that they had not been parentless orphans in need of a home as the Alabama couple had been told, but rather had been kidnapped from the orphanage where their mother had placed them temporarily and unwillingly put up for adoption.

"When I heard that I was flabbergasted," Desiree Smolin said. "I knew I had to keep moving forward and try to just keep these girls alive, but as a mother I knew we had to find their mother."

Nine months earlier the Smolins, already parents of five biological sons, had heard of the "millions of Indian orphans languishing and in need of a home" and decided to adopt difficult-to-place older girls.

Russell Goldman, "An Adoption Nightmare: An American Couple Adopted Indian Sisters, Only to Learn They'd Been Stolen," ABC News, May 14, 2008. Copyright © 2008 ABC News Internet Ventures. Reproduced by permission.

"The stories of female infanticide really got to us," Smolin said. "We perceived there was a great need and we wanted to share what we had. We loved being parents and we loved kids."

Smolin says the couple did their due diligence, finding a well-established agency and asking the questions they thought they were supposed to in order to determine everything was above board.

"We asked that the agency speak with the girls and make sure they wanted to be adopted," she said. "They assured us the girls wanted to be adopted and the mother had willingly signed them over. Unfortunately, much of what they told us would turn out to be false."

Problems Not Uncommon

The couple were told that Bhagya and Manjula were respectively 9 and 11 years old, but they now believe they are actually older.

When the girls arrived at the Atlanta airport in November 1998, they were just two of the 478 Indian orphans adopted by American families that year. In the years since, about 3,950 Indian orphans have found homes in the United States, according to State Department statistics.

Only [in 2008] did the United States implement the Hague Adoption Convention, which establishes international rules for vetting children to determine if they are true orphans and not the victims of kidnap.

Under the treaty, U.S. adoption agencies will for the first time be accredited by a national agency and have to register with the State Department.

About 19,613 children were adopted from foreign countries [in 2007], according to the State Department. The department does not keep statistics on how many visa applications are turned down for lack of proper documentation, or how many adoptees are ultimately discovered to have been kidnapped, but one official speaking on the condition of anonymity said such problems are unfortunately a fact of life.

"These issues come up and are not uncommon," said the official. "That is one of the reasons we joined Hague and encourage other countries to join the convention. In order for agencies to work in Hague partner countries, they have to be accredited by a U.S. body. Over 190 agencies have been accredited to determine that they properly review documents, make site visits and are legit."

Smolin and her husband adopted the girls before the Hague Convention was implemented and used an agency they believed took the proper steps to fully vet the orphanage and the girls. Smolin would not disclose the name of the agency she used.

By the time the girls arrived we knew that we had been lied to.

"We talked to a lot of people and found a well-respected agency. We thought we asked all the right questions. In the nine months it took for the adoption to be completed there were some things that worried us. In retrospect, had we known more about how international adoptions work we would have put the brakes on. We thought only ethical agencies could be in business and we thought they had checked out everything. We had faith in the system," she said.

"By the time the girls arrived we knew that we had been lied to."

Baby Buying

The Smolins later learned that the two orphanages in which the girls had lived near in Hyderabad were implicated in a far-reaching scandal.

Beginning in 1996, several orphanages, including the one in which the girls were placed, were accused of baby buying and falsifying documents. By 2001, after several scandals in Andahr Pradesh, the Indian government had banned all adoptions from that region.

Another American family's adopted Indian child who had lived with the girls at the orphanage revealed to her adoptive parents that the sisters had been stolen and unwillingly adopted.

When the Smolins confronted the girls, they broke down and admitted the story was true.

"The girls started crying and said the story was true. They had been threatened and forced to lie to the embassy official that interviewed them. Their mother had put them in an orphanage. It's not unusual for the poor to temporarily place their children in orphanages, which provide free education, housing, food and basic care, in a kind of boarding school setting."

When the family learned the truth, the girls had only been in the United States for six weeks. Immediately the family contacted the agency to conduct an investigation, but according to Smolin the agency did nothing of the kind.

We were made to feel bad and told that we were looking for a problem because we weren't committed.

"Had they investigated and found the mother we would have returned [the] girls. Instead, they denied the story could possibly be true," she said.

"The agency said they had double-checked right before the adoption went through and the mother had relinquished the girls, but when we asked them to check again—just six weeks later—they said they could no longer find her. Some in the adoptive community said the kids had made the story up to make themselves feel better and that parents sometimes stage a scene when they relinquish the children to trick them. We were made to feel bad and told that we were looking for a problem because we weren't committed."

The State Department does not comment on specific cases, but Ethica, a nonprofit agency that tracks ethical and legal problems in international adoptions, as well as an Indian researcher involved in locating the girls' mother, confirmed the Smolins' story.

A Few Bad Apples

Of the nearly 20,000 children adopted annually from outside the United States, most are legitimate orphans in need of loving homes, said Adam Pertman, executive director of the Evan B. Donaldson Adoption Institute, an adoption policy think tank.

"The truth is there are problems with the international adoption system. But American parents are often saving children from poverty, pestilence and war and we should not let the bad guys taint the good work many agencies are doing," he said. "If there is one child kidnapped and adopted, that is one too many. I can't speak about every adoption, and bad stuff does occur, but the majority are above board."

"Parents need to be careful. They need to be good consumers—not consumers of children, but of services. Too many people get so caught up in getting a child that they miss the red flags," he said.

The truth is there are problems with the international adoption system.

On the whole, India is not one of the more problematic countries, said a State Department official on the condition of anonymity. Adoptions from India peaked in 1998, the year the girls were adopted, and have been slowly on the decline, mirroring an overall downturn in foreign adoptions.

It took a year to settle the girls emotionally and get them into school. It would be an additional six years before the girls—then women in their own right and very much acclimated to America—would be reunited with their birth mother.

"Through e-mail and other contacts, various people told us they would help us locate the girls' first mother. We had the full name of their mother, father and brother and we knew the name of their ancestral village. Every time we thought we were close to finding their first mother, the trail would go cold."

In November 2004, local activist Gita Ramaswamy tracked down the [girls'] mother, and a year later, the older of the two, Manjula, visited her in India.

"When I found the girls' mother, Lakshmi, and told her that her daughters were alive and well and looking for her, she wept for a long time," Ramaswamy told ABCNEWS.com from Hyderabad. "I couldn't speak. I was overwhelmed. Lakshmi could not stop weeping—it was a dam that had burst. She was so keen to see them, to speak with them."

"One hears crazy stories like this in India all the time. The girls' story sounded authentic and when I had first confirmed it with another relative, and then met with Lakshmi, I knew they had been taken."

Ramaswamy was at the December 2005 reunion when Manjula saw her mother for the first time in six years.

"It was very emotional. Manjula was quiet, but the mother was very vocal. We Indians in time of grief and great happiness sing songs, and Lakshmi began to sing and chant. She chanted about how she gave birth and lost her girls, how she didn't know where they were and how she was reunited with them."

The following year, after she turned 18, Bhagya also returned to India to visit her birth mother.

Reunited

"It was just an incredible reunion. By that the time the girls were different people. They had become Americanized and were used to all our modern comforts. They feared what would happen if they went back, would they have to live in the village, would they be married off," Smolin said.

Neither Manjula nor Bhagya wanted to be interviewed by ABCNEWS.com, but Smolin said they both continue to live in the United States.

"We and the girls are still in close touch with their Indian family. We are a part of their life and they are a part of ours," she said.

Smolin now operates a Web site, in which she catalogs international adoption injustices and offers advice to adopting parents.

"Don't blindly trust your agency," she said. "Don't blindly trust the Hague convention. Do your homework. Dig for dirt. Love your kids."

More Adoption Regulations Are Needed to Prevent Potential Parents from Being Deceived

Michael Crowley

Michael Crowley is senior editor at The New Republic *magazine. He has contributed to* The New York Times Magazine, Slate, *and* The Atlantic.

Emotionally Crushed

A couple of years ago, Belinda Ramirez read an Internet adoption listing from Laura and Anthony Valois, a young New York couple who had been trying in vain to have their first child. Ramirez quickly contacted them from her home in Corpus Christi, Texas, telling them they could adopt her unborn baby. Excited, Laura and Anthony spent weeks communicating with Ramirez. They got regular updates on her pregnancy and even listened on the phone to what they were told was the baby's heartbeat on a fetal monitor.

Before long, Ramirez began asking them for financial support, like rent money. That took the Valoises by surprise. But they were willing to do a lot to ensure a smooth birth, including sending more than $1,000 to Ramirez over several months. Laura and Anthony finally drove to Texas so they could be on hand for the birth. But once they arrived, Ramirez gave them the runaround, avoiding their daily phone calls. After three weeks, the couple drove back to New York—empty-handed and emotionally crushed.

They later learned Ramirez had been bilking about ten other people, in states ranging from California to Ohio to

Florida, for such things as Wal-Mart gift cards that she said she needed for prenatal vitamins and maternity clothing. From start to finish, it was a scam. In fact, Ramirez was never even pregnant. In January she was sentenced to 24 months in prison without parole on charges of mail and wire fraud.

"When you find out you can't have children, it's just devastating," Laura Valois told a Texas TV station. "But when somebody intentionally does this to you, it's 15 times worse."

Adoption laws and standards vary from state to state, and can open the door to predators and scam artists.

This is one of the lowest scams around, masterminded by sleazy people who rip off couples looking to open their hearts and homes to an unwanted child. These swindlers target victims of an adoption system that can be so invasive, demanding, expensive and slow that the idea of bypassing the red tape is almost irresistible.

Advocates like Lee Allen of the National Council for Adoption (NCFA) stress that the process ensures legitimate adoptions are safe and well supervised. That's absolutely true. Still, adoption laws and standards vary from state to state, and can open the door to predators and scam artists. "The adoption industry operates with less regulation and consumer protection than your neighborhood health club," says Trish Maskew of Ethica, a nonprofit that promotes "ethical adoptions."

For Love, Not Money

That helps explain a scam that turned up in the Chicago area last year. Bill and Debra Klima spent seven months scamming thousands of dollars in free rent and other cash payments from adoption agencies to which they promised to give a child. One couple looked at ultrasound images of the baby and even went bowling with the Klimas. The racket came to light only when two people working for separate adoption agencies ran into each other and learned they were both helping the Klimas pay their rent.

Then there are scams involving the actual delivery of real children to adoptive parents. A Hawaiian woman named Lauryn Galindo worked as an adoption "facilitator," connecting would-be parents with children for a fee that usually ran over $10,000 per child. In Hawaii, as in many states, facilitators are not licensed, nor do they need special training. From 1997 to 2001, Galindo arranged some 800 adoptions of supposed Cambodian orphans in the United States—and got rich along the way, living in a $1.4 million home and driving a Jaguar.

Clearly, we need more checks and safeguards over the adoption process.

But Galindo's life in the fast lane came to a screeching halt when some of her adoptive parents discovered their children weren't orphans at all. The kids had living parents back in Cambodia. Even more shocking, some had sold their babies for as little as $15. One American parent later said her blood ran cold as she read a newspaper article about a Cambodian mother who'd been coerced into giving up her baby—and realized it was her newly adopted son, Sam. In November 2004, Galindo was sentenced to 18 months in prison for visa fraud and money laundering.

Cambodia is now closed to U.S. adoptions, but that leaves other hunting grounds for the slimeballs of the adoption trade. A recent 135-count federal indictment against Utah adoption agency Focus on Children alleges it tricked parents in the island nation of Samoa into giving up dozens of children for adoption by Americans. Birth parents who speak poor English reportedly signed away legal rights to their children without realizing what they were doing. (The agency's owners, who allegedly made hundreds of thousands of dollars, have denied the charges.)

Clearly we need more checks and safeguards over the adoption process. The United States has taken more than ten years to implement an international treaty imposing minimum standards on overseas adoptions, including a requirement that adoptions can be made only through officially accredited agencies. Those regulations are supposed to go into effect next year but won't include a number of popular adoption countries, like Vietnam, that haven't signed on to it.

Here at home, 12 states have taken a step that others should emulate: They forbid anyone other than state agencies and licensed businesses from advertising adoption services, whether on websites or in newspapers. Facilitators should also be licensed by the state to ensure they understand adoption laws and procedures. And, according to NCFA's Lee Allen, couples would be wise to hire an adoption attorney, and they should never use the Internet to adopt directly from a mother.

Above all, let's remember how joyous adoption can be, and take heart from people like Bob Temple and his wife, Alette Coble-Temple. This California couple spent a year trying to become parents before falling for the ruse of an Oregon woman who took thousands from them on the false promise they could adopt her unborn daughter.

But the story didn't end there. Another Oregon woman, eight months pregnant, had been thinking about giving up her baby. After watching a TV news story about Bob and Alette's case, she patted her belly and said to her unborn child, "I found your family." The adoption of Kathryn Taylor Temple went through without a hitch. The birth mother had just one request: She wanted her daughter to know that she had given her up out of love, not for money. If only everyone thought that way.

America's Adoption System Is Effective Because It Is Not Overregulated

Caitriona Palmer

Caitriona Palmer is a regular contributor to the online edition of The Irish Independent, *in which the following viewpoint appeared.*

When Faith Allen wanted to adopt a baby, she turned to the yellow pages. Allen, 37, a professional writer from North Carolina in the US, had suffered many painful years of infertility and in 1999 decided to adopt.

A friend recommended a nearby adoption agency but the three- to five-year waiting period seemed much too long to wait. That's when Allen decided to turn to the phone book.

"I wound up stumbling upon a wonderful agency," said Allen who admits that she "got lucky" with her find.

Nearly two years and $12,000 (E8,000 [euros]) later, Allen's dearest wish was finally realised when she became a mother to a little baby boy named Nicholas.

Unlike Ireland and Britain, adoption in the United States tends to be a faster process.

When news of his birth broke, Allen and her husband packed their car and drove six hours from North Carolina to Georgia. For two days they waited anxiously in a friend's house until the baby's mother signed the papers. Three days after his birth, they had Nicholas in their arms.

Allen's long but successful journey to parenthood is a typical story of American adoption. Although the number of available babies in the United States has declined in recent years, many states, particularly those in the South, seem to have a healthy pool of available children.

Faster, but More Expensive

Unlike Ireland and Britain, adoption in the United States tends to be a faster process, where adoptive parents can be paired with a birth mother earlier—during her pregnancy. But adopting an American baby is a more expensive proposition mainly because private agencies must charge for services that would be bankrolled by the state in Europe.

British Foreign Secretary David Miliband and his US-born wife Louise recently adopted a newborn baby boy from America—their second adopted son from the country. According to Miliband, his wife's nationality made America an obvious choice. But speedier adoption services in the United States must also have been an incentive.

For those eager to adopt in America, the initial steps can be just a click away. Privatised agencies staffed by child welfare social workers advertise openly on the web, attracting potential clients with savvy slogans and guarantees of "delivery within four months".

With costs ranging from $20,000 to $35,000, nearly anyone—single, married or gay—can offer a child a home. As long, of course, as they can afford the fees, pass intensive home-study assessments and background checks, and compete for the attention of their would-be children's birth parents. The thriving adoption sector in the US might seem an extension of America's insatiable consumerist appetite, but experts say that babies are definitely not for sale.

"Americans aren't out baby buying, which is what too many people perceive us as being," said Adam Pertman, the executive director of the Evan B. Donaldson Adoption Institute in New York and author of *Adoption Nation*. "They are overwhelmingly providing homes for kids who really need them. And I'm not sure what the downside to that is." Pertman said that the massive agency fees cover the costs of essential services—services that are provided free to those engaged in domestic adoptions in Ireland.

"It's not done through any federal or state financing. Somebody has to pay for all that—all those medical services, social services, counseling services and social workers' salaries," he said.

"That goes a long way towards explaining why there is so much money involved. Sometimes we overpay for those services . . . sometimes those services are eminently reasonable. But they're services," he said.

Restrictions in the UK and Ireland

The situation in the US differs greatly from the struggling domestic adoption system in Ireland and Britain where the availability of contraception and the lessening stigma against single parenthood has seen the number of available children—particularly babies—slow to a mere trickle in the past decade.

In 2005, 253 domestic adoption orders were made in Ireland—the majority of which were 'family adoptions' involving stepchildren. Consequently the majority of Irish parents eager to adopt must look towards other countries, particularly China, Russia, Vietnam and Thailand.

"Currently the two most popular countries are Russia and Vietnam," said Derek Cregan, co-chair of the Inter-country Adoption Association in Ireland and a father to two young boys adopted from Russia. "China is open for adoption, as is India, Thailand and the Philippines. But they're all very slow."

According to a spokesperson from the International Adoption Association in Dublin, the waiting times for Irish parents wishing to adopt abroad vary considerably.

"We are aware that the total period from expression of interest to completion of assessments, and receiving a declaration from the Adoption Board can amount to four or five years," she said.

In Britain, the situation for prospective parents who wish to adopt children within the country is equally bleak.

Less than 4,000 children are adopted there each year out of 80,000 in care. And strict restrictions on exactly who can adopt mean that many British couples—particularly those over 40—are forced to adopt internationally.

International Adoptions

In the US, the paltry welfare system reportedly makes it hard for many poor single parents to contemplate keeping their children. In the case of Nicholas, according to Allen, his birth father was no longer in the picture and his mother—despite being in her thirties—recognised that her baby needed more than she could offer.

"Her life circumstances were such that she was working two jobs and had very little time available for raising a baby," said Allen.

In the US, adoptive parents are also obliged to pay some expenses for the biological mother during her pregnancy, which can range widely depending on her circumstances.

Approximately 800 American children a year find a home and a family with citizens from other countries such as Canada, Mexico and France.

"In the state in which we adopted, expecting mothers may only be paid money for medical expenses, housing and food, and even those amounts have a cap. Our agency said that the average request for funds is $2,000, but my son's birthmother only requested one bag of groceries," Allen said.

Irish families who wish to adopt privately from the US are free to do so, according to Thomas DiFilipo, president of the Joint Council on International Children's Services in Virginia. "Approximately 800 American children a year find a home and a family with citizens from other countries such as Canada, Mexico and France," said DiFilipo.

There are no citizenship or residency requirements but prospective Irish parents would have to undergo the same procedures as any American family in addition to registering with the adoption board in Ireland.

Regardless of the rules, adoption is often full of uncertainty.

"From the day I decided I wanted to become a mother to the day I became one, four-and-a-half years passed," said Allen. "That was five Christmases and four Mother's Days with empty arms. That was the hardest part."

China's New Adoption Regulations Will Prevent Many Americans from Adopting Children

Elisa Poncz

Attorney Elisa Poncz is an associate with Morgan Lewis in Philadelphia.

China's new international adoption law, [which took] effect on May 1, 2007, will prohibit international adoption of Chinese children by single adults. International adoption is a popular avenue for prospective adoptive parents in the United States, and because China has been a major source of internationally adopted children, these new laws will significantly impact the steady trend of U.S. citizens adopting abroad. It is unlikely that China's more stringent adoption requirements will affect U.S. domestic adoption policies even though the requirements will hinder adoption by some U.S. prospective parents. Accordingly, United States citizens who cannot meet the new Chinese adoption standards will have to adopt less "adoptable" children, look to other sender-countries, pursue options like reproductive technology, or decide to forego parenthood altogether.

I begin by examining the specifics of China's proposed international adoption law and China's international adoption policies. Next, I briefly consider China's role as a significant sender-country to the United States. Finally, I explore the likely impact of the Chinese tightening adoption standards on

Elisa Poncz, "China's Proposed International Adoption Law: The Likely Impact on Single U.S. Citizens Seeking to Adopt from China and the Available Alternatives," *Harvard International Law Journal*, vol. 48, April 29, 2007, pp. 74–82. Copyright © 2007 by the President and Fellows of Harvard College. Reproduced by permission.

potential U.S. adoptive parents, looking specifically at the alternatives that the parents who will no longer be able to adopt from China can pursue.

China's New International Adoption Law

The proposed new international adoption policies will join a set of preexisting standards for both foreign and domestic prospective adopters in China. Since enacted in 1991, China's adoption standards have operated according to a sliding scale depending on the characteristics of the children available for adoption. Other preexisting limitations include an outright ban on adoption by homosexuals, a suggested monetary contribution to the institution caring for the adopted child, and a minimum two-week stay in China prior to adoption. China's 1991 adoption policies restricted domestic adoptions to childless Chinese citizens over age 35.

Through the 1990s and 2000s, international adoption has been a major source of adoption for Chinese children. This, coupled with the stringent domestic requirements enacted in 1991, may have indicated a preference on the part of Chinese officials for international adoption over domestic adoption. Since the early 1990s, however, China has lifted some of the restrictions on domestic adoptions. Accordingly, although precise numbers are not available, it is likely that domestic Chinese adoptions have increased.

China explains the tightened international adoption policy by positing that there are fewer babies available for adoption from China because of increased domestic adoption and a loosened "one-child" policy.

The preliminary version of the May 1, 2007 requirements for international adoption from China adds new requirements for international adoptive parents. Among other restrictions and stipulations, the new requirements prohibit single individuals from adopting:

Prospective adoptive parents must be married for at least two years (marriage is defined as being between a man and a woman). If either the husband or wife has been divorced (no more than two divorces), the prospective adoptive parents must be married for at least five years.

The new requirements also focus on physical attributes—banning adoption by prospective parents whose body mass index is greater than 40, who take psychotic medicines for disorders like depression, mania, or anxiety-neurosis, and who are blind in one or both eyes.

China explains the tightened international adoption policy by positing that there are fewer babies available for adoption from China because of increased domestic adoption and a loosened "one-child" policy. Yet, the increase in domestic adoptions has unlikely been significant enough to provide homes for the large numbers of Chinese children in orphanages. If there actually are fewer babies available for adoption, the decrease may be a result of troubling social practices (like gender-specific abortion) and not the end of the abandonment practices that previously filled the orphanages. For example, even though gender-specific abortion is officially illegal in China, the country's birth rate is very unbalanced: For every 100 girls, 120 boys are born. In addition, it is estimated that China might be missing some 40 to 60 million women by 2012. . . .

Such skepticism over China's assertion that there simply is not an excess supply of children waiting in institutions for adoption is fueled by various accounts of steady levels of Chinese babies in orphanages.

China as a Key Sender-Country

Single individuals often pursue international adoption because of the difficulties for them in adopting within the United States. U.S. adoption policy is a state-based system, and states impose high thresholds for parental screening. Most interactions between U.S. citizens and the government cannot involve discrimination on the basis of age, race, and marital status, but adoption can involve these types of discrimination. [Harvard law professor] Elizabeth Bartholet describes the plight of a potential adoptive parent in the United States:

> Those who would adopt have no rights. They must beg for the privilege of parenting, and do so in a state-administered realm that denies them both the right to privacy and the 'civil rights' that we have come to think of as fundamental in the rest of our communal life.

The difficulties posed by such discrimination push some U.S. prospective adoptive parents to adopt abroad.

China has been a main source of foreign adoptive children for U.S. adoptive parents. Between 1985 and 2006, 62,389 children were adopted to the United States from China. One of the main reasons why China has been an attractive sender-country is the abundance of healthy baby girls abandoned to orphanages due to China's one-child policy. As a result of the large number of Chinese children adopted in the United States, a support community of adopted Chinese children and their adoptive families has developed. This community might make adoption from China more attractive to U.S. adoptive parents. These factors, coupled with the growing awareness of international adoption, have given China the preeminent position among source countries for U.S. adoption.

Single individuals often pursue international adoption because of the difficulties for them in adopting within the United States.

The centralization of adoption by the Chinese government through an agency called the China Center for Adoption Affairs (CCAA) has helped to organize, regulate, and foster international adoption from China. The creation of such a centralized body is one of the key recommendations of the Hague Convention to help protect children in sender-countries and to discourage corruption, baby buying, and kidnapping. Indeed, the Chinese government's tight grip on international adoption through the CCAA has kept adoption from China virtually corruption-free, whereas other nations grapple with a variety of problems that plague their adoption systems. When adoption practices within a sender-country seem corrupt, receiving nations, like the Untied States, usually put a moratorium on adoption from these countries.

Even though the CCAA helps to keep China's international adoption corruption-free, it also is the source of the new Chinese international adoption regulations. Ironically, then, the organization creating stricter policies that will limit the ability of U.S. citizens to adopt in China is one of the reasons that China has been such an attractive sender-country in the past.

The Impact on U.S. Adoptions

If the preliminary version of the new Chinese international adoption law is implemented, it will prohibit adoptions by single individuals in the United States. This will likely impact many groups of prospective adoptive parents, such as homosexuals who previously could subvert prohibitions on homosexual adoption from China by adopting as single individuals. Far from being an anomaly in adoption law, China's prohibition on homosexual adoption parallels Florida's policies, found constitutional by the Eleventh Circuit in *Lofton v. Sec'y of the Dep't of Children and Family Servs.* Much like China's policy that "foreign homosexuals are not allowed to adopt children in China," Florida's adoption law has "contained a codified prohibition on adoption by any homosexual person" since 1977. The Eleventh Circuit allowed discrimination against prospective homosexual adoptive parents because adoption is regarded as distinct from other government-citizen interactions: "Because of the primacy of the welfare of the child, the state can make classifications for adoption purposes that would be constitutionally suspect in many other arenas." U.S. states' adoption policies do not rest on the assumption that those U.S. citizens unable to adopt domestically will be able to adopt abroad. So, even though homosexuals will have less opportunity to adopt children due to the stricter Chinese regulations, U.S. states will probably not respond by making adoption by homosexuals a stronger right at home because there is no right for U.S. prospective adoptive parents to adopt.

As I describe below, after the implementation of the new Chinese international adoption regulations, such groups (like homosexual individuals or couples eager to adopt) will have four main legal alternatives: (1) adopt children with medical problems and disabilities, (2) adopt children from other sender-countries, (3) pursue reproductive technology, and (4) eschew adoption altogether.

(1) Prospective adopters from the United States might circumvent China's new restrictions by adopting children with health problems, disabilities, or [as the *Wall Street Journal's* Geoffrey Fowler expressed it,] "minor birth defects that they think can be corrected in U.S. hospitals. . . ." As the Chinese policies demonstrate, the requirements for prospective adoptive parents for children with health issues are usually lower. For example, waiting periods tend to be shorter for children with health problems or disabilities. An increase in such adoptions may help to ensure that these children find homes, but it is important to consider that these homes (and parents) may not be equipped to handle the complexities that come with children who have serious health issues or disabilities.

U.S. singles might be deterred from adopting altogether when barred from adopting from China.

---

(2) More stringent international adoption policies in China might push U.S. citizens to adopt from alternative countries

(like Russia or Vietnam) that have different adoption criteria. The accessibility of specific sender-countries in international adoption tends to ebb and flow depending on the global political climate and domestic issues. Romania, for example, used to be a popular sender-country for international adoptions to the United States. Despite having many children in orphanages, Romania completely closed its borders to international adoption in 2001.

(3) Another alternative for U.S. singles seeking children is reproductive technology. The components necessary for reproduction are available on the open market in the United States, and besides monetary factors, there are few restrictions on access to these resources. Thus, homosexual couples and single individuals who cannot adopt readily abroad might instead choose to "make" a child. Unfortunately, an increase in reproductive technology means a decrease in people fighting to adopt existing children in need of homes around the world.

(4) Finally, U.S. singles might be deterred from adopting altogether when barred from adopting from China. This consequence would both prevent single would-be parents from experiencing parenthood and leave many children without the numerous benefits that a loving home could bring. Adults who want children and children who need parents would both exist—separate from each other and unable to form families.

No matter how many Chinese children remain in orphanages, the number of international adoptions from China will surely decrease because of these new regulations.

In the Best Interest of the Child

International adoption is a contentious issue. Child advocates voice concerns for the best interest of children on both sides of the debate. The proponents of international adoption argue that without international adoption these children will live out their lives in orphanages and on the streets. The opponents of international adoption argue that corruption robs sender-countries of their dignity and their most precious resource—the children themselves. There is also concern that while international adoption may have once provided a method for finding parents for children, it has transformed into a practice of finding children for parents. Recent international adoptions by headline celebrities have brought the discussion to the fore of public debate. The new Chinese adoption policies again stir the international adoption debate.

With these disagreements in mind, the new requirements from China could be a positive development if there *truly* are fewer children in need of homes. The small number of children would be able to be matched with parents that China deems most fit. China's assertion that there are drastically fewer babies available for adoption seems far-fetched, however, when considered in light of the incredible number of children that have previously filled China's orphanages. An exact number of children still waiting for homes in China is unavailable.

No matter how many Chinese children remain in orphanages, the number of international adoptions from China will surely decrease because of these new regulations. If China decides it only wants its children going to certain types of homes, then no one—not the United States, nor individual parents—can make China do otherwise. China's new regulations will be yet another obstacle in the distinctively sensitive realm of adoption. Adoption is already a difficult, expensive, and emotionally complex process, and now a country with what is in all likelihood a vast number of children languishing in orphanages has made adoption less likely. It is entirely possible that in light of these challenges individuals seeking the parenting experience would forgo it.

Even more troubling than the impact these regulations will have on prospective parents is the impact tighter regulations might have on un-adopted children. If China has fewer children awaiting homes, and if the new regulations do not prohibit families from adopting children who need homes, then the children are concededly no worse-off. If, on the other hand, these regulations prohibit even one child from being adopted, then in my opinion they will have failed.

Implementation of the Hague Convention Will Harm American Adoption Agencies and Potential Parents

Denise L. Behreandt

Denise L. Behreandt is a member of the The John Birch Society, a self-described conservative political organization, and a regular contributor to the society's publication The New American, *from which the following viewpoint was excerpted.*

Little Claudia Maria, born April 15, 2007, awaits adoption in Guatemala City. It is simply easy for anyone to gush or marvel at this cutie posted at www.adopting.com in the agency's "Waiting Child Photolisting." And it wouldn't take much enticement for someone wanting to adopt a beautiful baby girl to want to take Claudia home. Unfortunately, Claudia, and many of the other children presently available for adoption, will not be arriving at the homes of loving couples in the United States. This is due to the implementation of the Hague Convention on Intercountry Adoption (HCICA).

The Hague Conference on Private International Law, "a global inter-governmental organization which develops conventions (similar to treaties) promoting mutual agreement and compatible legal procedures among countries," developed the Hague Convention on Intercountry Adoption. In 2000, the U.S. Congress passed the Intercountry Adoption Convention bill into law. On November 16, 2007, President [George W.] Bush signed the U.S. instrument of ratification of the Hague Adoption Convention. The convention will go into force for the United States on April 1, 2008.

The Council of Accreditation, "an international, independent, not-for-profit, child- and family-service and behavioral healthcare accrediting organization," will be responsible for determining eligibility for adoption agencies or providers under eligibility rules established by the Hague Convention. Under this arrangement, "private adoption service providers will generally need to be accredited, temporarily accredited, or approved, or be supervised by a provider that is accredited, temporarily accredited, or approved, in order to provide adoption services in cases involving the United States and another Convention country." In other words, adoption and foster care providers must meet Hague approval before they can take part in intercountry adoption services.

No Permission Granted

The new Hague rules also mean that U.S. couples and agencies cannot work on adoptions from countries not party to the Hague Convention. One such country is Guatemala, a nation that lacks government infrastructure for compliance.

In Guatemala, private "notaries who work with birth mothers, determine if babies were surrendered willingly, hire foster mothers and handle all the paperwork," says MSNBC. U.S. parents adopted approximately 4,135 Guatemalan children [in 2007] with the help of notaries. The Hague Convention, even if it were adopted by Guatemala, would "reduce the number of Guatemalan adoptions because the government doesn't have the resources to manage all the cases that notaries have handled," MSNBC notes.

By [the Hague Convention's] drastically increasing the amount of government regulation of the adoption process, even U.S. adoption agencies face uncertain futures.

Guatemala, however, may not become party to the Hague agreement. So-called "non-Hague countries," like Guatemala, who were not party to the drafting of the Convention, must agree to it through accession. The Guatemala Adoptive Families Network, a group of people who have adopted children from Guatemala and provide support and awareness on the issue of Guatemalan adoptions, says that's not likely. According to the organization:

> The Guatemalan constitution does not permit accession to treaties, only ratification, and the terms under which Guatemala agreed to the Vienna Convention (which governs all international treaties) complicated this matter further. As a result the accession to HCICA was declared unconstitutional by Guatemala's Constitutional Court in August 2003, and adoptions then continued under the previous system. . . . Within Guatemala the legal view seems to be that Guatemala is not a Hague country, and cannot become one. However, because Guatemala's original accession was properly documented under international legal standards, and Guatemala did not withdraw from HCICA when the accession was declared unconstitutional, under international law Guatemala is considered a Hague country by the Hague Conference and by other countries, including the US.

Although the United States may consider Guatemala a Hague country, prospective U.S. parents still would not be allowed to adopt Guatemalan children because agencies will not be able to legally process adoptions until Hague-compliant procedures are in place in Guatemala.

Big Government

By drastically increasing the amount of government regulation of the adoption process, even U.S. adoption agencies face uncertain futures. Many agencies are already scrambling to keep their doors open due to the burdensome accreditation process. Leonette Boirski, director of the adoption agency Welcome House, pleads with individuals on the agency's website to write letters to the Council of Accreditation and the Department of State, asking them to reduce the accreditation fees. In her appeal for help, she writes:

> Recently, the accrediting body that will be responsible for assessing all agencies across the US, the Council of Accreditation (COA), reported that they are planning to propose a fee range of $8,000 to $22,000, plus the cost of a site visit (estimated at dollar;5,000) to the Department of State. The fee for a specific agency will be based upon their budget. Throughout the process of implementing the Hague in the United States, COA and the Department of State have assured agencies that the costs for accreditation would be fairly minimal. Welcome House set aside what we thought would be a sufficient amount for accreditation, but our estimate is thousands short of what COA is proposing.

Some agencies won't survive the cost associated with these regulations; others will, but only after paying a heavy price. David Ptasnik is co-director of the for-profit agency Americans Adopting Orphans. According to the adoption site, www.adopting.org:

> Ptasnik admits that his agency could survive the financial burden of accreditation, but says that many others could not. Giving some numbers, he says, "I estimate it will take at least $20,000 in staff time to complete, the fee to the COA will be somewhere between $7,000 and $10,000. I will have to buy at least $5,000 more insurance than our agency currently carries, and I will probably have to change the corporate nature of our company, with the result of losing perhaps as much as $250,000 in effective assets."

The agency will have to become a nonprofit organization to gain accreditation. No longer will business owners like Ptasnik be able to determine the nature of the organization. Currently, there are very many children who need to be adopted into loving homes, and these regulations may either prevent or impede the adoption process for many of them. And prospective parents will have to absorb the costs associated with the new regulations.

Because of international big government, fewer needy children will be helped and fewer happy families will be created, leaving children like Claudia Maria victims of big government.

CHAPTER 2

What Risks and Benefits May Accompany International Adoptions?

Chapter Preface

According to The National Center on Family Homelessness, during any given year up to 1.35 million U.S. children are homeless. While a percentage of these children, some along with their families, are only temporarily homeless, thousands of children remain in the foster care and adoption system throughout the country. Given the number of dispossessed children, many people wonder why potential parents would choose to adopt children from other nations, especially since www.adoption.com reveals it can cost nothing to adopt a child in state custody as opposed to upwards of forty thousand dollars for international adoptions.

Some parents choose to adopt children from other countries because they believe it lowers the risks of future complications. In an article in the *Indianapolis Star*, Courtenay Edelhart and T.J. Banes write, "Some worry that a birth mother in this country may change her mind after placing a child for adoption." Adopting children from other nations reduces this risk because the birth parents are far away and because the legal rights to the adopted children are better regulated. It is easier, some adoptive parents believe, for U.S. birth parents to have their children returned to them should they change their minds.

On the other hand, children from other lands can grow up to long for their birth parents and may feel estranged from their homelands. Chris Atkins, a social worker who helps adopted children adjust, was adopted from Hong Kong by white parents. She says this of her own struggles to adapt to a different culture: "There is the feeling of displacement, the constant challenge to fit in somewhere, and it lasts a lifetime." She also notes that she "worked with adult transnational adoptees who have suffered breakdowns, have problems with relationships, and have huge issues with their identity." There is a sense, according to Atkins, of never quite belonging anywhere.

Despite these challenges, the majority of international adoptions seem to be beneficial to both adoptive parents and adoptees. Potential parents go through a rigorous screening process, including home studies that can take up to three months to complete. In general, children from other lands are in desperate need of safe, healthy homes as orphanages become overcrowded. Harvard University law professor Elizabeth Bartholet writes, "The poor countries of the world have long had an excess of children for whom they cannot adequately care—children doomed to grow up in grossly inadequate orphanages or on the streets." Few people would deny these children the right to grow up happy and well cared for.

In the end, it is difficult to know the best interests of all parties involved. Children all over the world need homes. At the same time, restrictions enforced by U.S. adoption agencies often encourage potential adoptive parents to seek children beyond their own borders. Surely, the debate about how best to regulate international adoptions will continue. As the authors in this chapter make clear, the best interests of children must be kept at the forefront.

International Adoptions Should Adhere to the Hague Convention

The United Nations Children's Fund

The United Nations Children's Fund (UNICEF) is an international organization that strives to protect the world's children.

UNICEF has received many enquiries from families hoping to adopt children from countries other than their own. UNICEF believes that all decisions relating to children, including adoptions, should be made with the best interests of the child as the primary consideration. The Hague Convention on International Adoptions is an important development, for both adopting families and adopted children, because it promotes ethical and transparent processes, undertaken in the best interests of the child. UNICEF urges national authorities to ensure that, during the transition to full implementation of the Hague Convention, the best interests of each individual child are protected.

The Convention on the Rights of the Child, which guides UNICEF's work, clearly states that every child has the right to know and be cared for by his or her own parents, whenever possible. Recognising this, and the value and importance of families in children's lives, UNICEF believes that families needing support to care for their children should receive it, and that alternative means of caring for a child should only be considered when, despite this assistance, a child's family is unavailable, unable or unwilling to care for him or her.

For children who cannot be raised by their own families, an appropriate alternative family environment should be sought in preference to institutional care which should be

The United Nations Children's Fund, "UNICEF's Position on Inter-Country Adoption," UNICEF, October 21, 2008. Reproduced by permission.

used only as a last resort and as a temporary measure. Inter-country adoption is one of a range of care options which may be open to children, and for individual children who cannot be placed in a permanent family setting in their countries of origin, it may indeed be the best solution. In each case, the best interests of the individual child must be the guiding principle in making a decision regarding adoption.

UNICEF believes that all decisions relating to children, including adoptions, should be made with the best interest of the child as the primary consideration.

Over the past 30 years, the number of families from wealthy countries wanting to adopt children from other countries has grown substantially. At the same time, lack of regulation and oversight, particularly in the countries of origin, coupled with the potential for financial gain, has spurred the growth of an industry around adoption, where profit, rather than the best interests of children, takes centre stage. Abuses include the sale and abduction of children, coercion of parents, and bribery.

Many countries around the world have recognised these risks, and have ratified the Hague Convention on Inter-Country Adoption. UNICEF strongly supports this international legislation, which is designed to put into action the principles regarding inter-country adoption which are contained in the Convention on the Rights of the Child. These include ensuring that adoption is authorised only by competent authorities, that inter-country adoption enjoys the same safeguards and standards which apply in national adoptions, and that inter-country adoption does not result in improper financial gain for those involved in it. These provisions are meant first and foremost to protect children, but also have the positive effect of providing assurance to prospective adoptive parents that their child has not been the subject of illegal and detrimental practices.

The case of children separated from their parents and communities during war or natural disasters merits special mention. It cannot be assumed that such children have neither living parents nor relatives. Even if both their parents are dead, the chances of finding living relatives, a community and home to return to after the conflict subsides exist. Thus, such children should not be considered for inter-country adoption, and family tracing should be the priority. This position is shared by UNICEF, UNHCR [United Nations High Commissioner for Refugees], the International Confederation of the Red Cross, and international NGOs [nongovernmental organizations] such as the Save the Children Alliance.

International Adoption Can Benefit Older Potential Parents

Marie Pruden

Marie Pruden is a former Wall Street executive. She currently works in her husband's oral surgery practice.

In November, 2004, my husband Peter and I went to Tomsk, Siberia, Russia, to adopt Anastasia—age 10, James—age 10, and Alexander—age 9, who were all in an orphanage for 4 years. The boys are brothers and the girl is a friend.

It's funny because I feel like this happens to other people that you read about in the papers. But now I am living the story.

You are probably wondering how this all started? Well, my husband Peter, who is actually the fourth kid at heart and in life, planted the seed. Peter loves kids. He is ready to be Santa at Christmas, go to an amusement park or movie on a moment's notice, even on a school night. He does zany things and thinks like a child.

We got married at age 38 and could not have children even with technology's help. We accepted the fact, and continued along with our lifestyle of being first born, workaholics and house renovators. We also enjoyed spending time with all our family and friends. This went on for 15 years.

Occasionally, Peter would suggest to me that we should go to China and adopt an infant baby girl. I always looked at him like he had two heads. How was I going to take care of an infant and continue working on Wall Street? I eventually quit my job after 21 years, and have been working in Peter's office for the last 10 years, still in workaholic fashion.

Marie Pruden, "Patience and Leap of Faith Overcame Infertility and Fears of Parenthood," International Adoption Articles Directory, April 26, 2006. Reproduced by permission of the author.

Time passed and then Life threw in twists and turns. Within the last few years, we saw Peter's mother die suddenly of breast cancer. My dear father who had heart disease became increasingly sicker, and died right after the children came home. I knew he hung in there to see them. We saw our nieces and nephews grow older. And we experienced some business difficulties.

How was I going to take care of an infant and continue working on Wall Street?

Each of us began to reassess things in general unbeknownst to the other.

Then one day, Peter, who is an oral surgeon, was treating the last patient of the night. She blurted out to him, "You look sad", and then asked why. In his usual, honest style he said, "I have no children". She said, "You look like the father of three". She told Peter and then I that she read in the Huntington [New York] church bulletin about a summer program to host older children from Russia on a trial basis with the hopes of adoption. Neither Peter nor I said anything about it to each other.

Researching Adoption

A week passed and one night after work, I asked Peter if he wanted to go to his college alumni dinner or the adoption meeting in town. He immediately said, "The alumni dinner can't help us." And off we went.

At the end of the adoption seminar, the speaker asked any interested parties to come forward and complete an application to be a summer host. I looked at Peter and said, "What should we do?" He gave me a St. Michael the Archangel coin which had an inscription on the back that said, "Rise up and meet your challenges".

Peter is a quiet soul and always said, "God had a plan for us". I would ask him what is the plan? He would say, you need to get quiet and listen. I was fearful, but I began to think children were part of the plan.

The mounds of adoption paperwork began. You truly needed a PhD in adoption. Peter said, let's do it quickly because he had a sneaking suspicion that the Russian government was going to halt adoptions. So we did. It was April 2004.

Choosing the Right Children

The adoption facilitator helped us select a girl, Anastasia. She dropped off her picture and placed it under our front door mat with her half page of information. We decided to go ahead with Anastasia.

We wanted to get two children and started to inquire about a boy. But the adoption agency said that there were no single boys left at Anastasia's orphanage, only siblings. (In Russia, prospective parents have to adopt multiple children from the same orphanage).

I went to a pre-adoption meeting, and there was a table of pictures of unassigned children. Somehow I moved toward the table and immediately picked up the picture of two brothers who happened to be in Anastasia's orphanage. I was drawn to their faces, and brought the picture home to show Peter. I said, "These boys are adorable, but we can't adopt 3 children". Peter said, "Why not, of course we can". We then decided to host all of them for the summer of 2004.

We told our family at Easter Sunday Dinner and everyone was excited and supportive. I will never forget the look on my Dad's face. He was surprised and happy. He said, "Great, Marie, Congratulations". Our patient, Linda, who started the ball rolling as God's messenger, was also thrilled.

But then we began to think we lost our minds, three kids in our 50's! The monsignor at our church said, "Peter, less is more." So after much agonizing thought, we both agreed and told the agency that we would just host the girl.

Well, as luck would have it, Linda, the patient came back for a follow up visit. Peter told her we decided to just host Anastasia. She looked Peter straight in the eye, and said, "Do you want those two boys?" He of course said, "Yes". We changed our minds again.

It became very clear that there was a reason that 15 years had passed us by without any children.

Meeting the Children

We decided that God has a plan with perfect timing which is predestined. It was no accident that this series of events led us to our family. The three kids came for the three weeks in summer of 2004 and all went very well. They called us Momma and Poppa. We called them the munchkins.

They spoke Russian. We spoke English. After three weeks, we knew that God selected these children for us, and selected us as parents for these children. It became very clear that there was a reason that 15 years had passed us by without any children.

They returned to northern Siberia, in a town called Kolpashevo, while the paperwork was being finalized.

Now the day arrived!! November 11, 2004. We were leaving for Siberia for two weeks to bring the munchkins home. We boarded the plane from JFK [International Airport in New York City] to Moscow and it took 10 plus hours. We stayed one night in Moscow, and went to another airport to get on a 10 pm flight to Tomsk, Siberia. This flight took 6 hours.

It was a small, old plane with ripped, plaid seat covers and lots of Russian people talking loudly. I was nervous, and scared, and felt like I was in a movie. Peter was taking it all in. It was an adventure. Peter was also busy writing a journal, which he continued throughout the trip. One hour before we were about to land in the dark coldness, Peter turned to me and said, "I always knew God would give me children, I just didn't know how".

The plane landed and we descended the steps onto the frozen tarmac as it was snowing. It was 4 am. I got a hot flash, my heart was palpitating. I stopped in my tracks as we walked to the small building to get our luggage.

I told Peter that I was frightened and this was the scariest thing we ever did. I said, "Let's turn around and get back on the plane". He grabbed my hand and said, "Everything will be all right".

We arrived at the small pensione hotel in Tomsk, Siberia, at 5 am and went right to sleep. A few hours later, the phone rang and then came a knock at the door two minutes later. The three munchkins were standing side-by-side all bundled up with the Director of the Orphanage who had brought them to us. I will never forget their faces dressed in orphanage clothes and excited to see us; just as excited as we were to see them.

Then we went to court where a judge had a proceeding where she questioned us for three and one half hours. The children also testified. James said he wanted to go to America to get a good education and a good job; Alex said he was already in America in his mind; and Anastasia said we were the only parents she ever knew. We all celebrated after the judge granted us permission to adopt.

Taking Them Home

We flew back to Moscow and hired a tour guide who was a translator. In the Kremlin Museum, the tour guide showed the children all the icons, and said that Momma and Poppa were praying for children of their own. The children told the guide that they were also praying for a Momma and Poppa to come and get them.

We arrived home on the night before Thanksgiving, 2004. And it has been a whirlwind ever since; a process of becoming a family that continues to evolve every day. Now, I know how hard our parents worked at raising us and loving us. And I am amazed every day by what they did, and am forever grateful. Thank you Mom and Dad. . . .

Our families and friends have been a constant source of support and help during this transition and adjustment for all of us. It seems like we always had kids. They do bring a lot of joy and a lot of work. And the children have come to know what an extended circle of love means: Grandma, Aunts, Uncles, Sisters, Brothers, Cousins and Dear Friends.

Immediately after their arrival, we got the children tested by a well-known Russian/American psychologist, Dr. Boris Gindis, whose expertise focuses on internationally adopted children. He helped us deal with school and emotional issues. After testing the children for two days, Dr. Gindis sat back and looked at us. He said there was nothing wrong with the children, but he wanted to know what was wrong with us for adopting three at one time when we were 52!

There are many childless couples or couples who want to expand their family, and adoption could be a possibility.

To keep our sanity, we hired a translator and had family meetings every week. We also have a tutor come after school 4 days a week and hired household help.

The kids thrived and learned English and are now speaking fluently. They made school friends, play sports, have sleepovers, go to summer camp and have had several family vacations. They are kids like all others: they laugh, scream, cry, fight, yell, and give you a kiss when you least expect it and are trying to find themselves. These kids are survivors and adapt easily. They have experienced many new firsts, and so have we through their eyes.

But most of all they are kids who no longer have the worry of abandonment by alcoholic, drug addicted parents, nor the worry of food or shelter, as they lived in non-heated huts with dirt floors and plastic windows in Siberia. There are over 700,000 of these children in Russia alone.

There are many childless couples or couples who want to expand their family, and adoption could be a possibility. For me, it only became one when I allowed myself to take a big leap of faith and move out of my comfort zone. As [American novelist] Willa Cather said, "Miracles surround us at every turn, if we but sharpen our perception of them".

International Adoption Can Be a Viable Option for African Orphans

Jini L. Roby and Stacey A. Shaw

Jini L. Roby is an associate professor of social work at Brigham Young University in Provo, Utah. Stacey A. Shaw is an independent researcher who studies the orphan crisis in Africa.

The orphan crisis in sub-Saharan Africa has reached desperate proportions. In a region racked with civil war, poverty, and diseases, 12.3 million children have lost one or both parents to AIDS, and orphan numbers are projected to rise to 18.4 million by 2010. With 25 million people in the region living with AIDS, overall infection rates are more than 20 percent in seven countries and reach 38 percent in some areas. Although adult prevalence rates in the region appear to have stabilized, AIDS claimed 2.2 million lives, and 3 million people became infected in 2003. The full impact of the AIDS pandemic hits the hardest in the lives of young children. Although only 10 percent of the world's population live in sub-Saharan Africa, nearly 80 percent of the world's AIDS orphans come from this area. Each orphaned child has a story and a life.

Although the orphan crisis has been building for more than a decade, the global response has been slow and unorganized. In 2001 Carol Bellamy, executive director of UNICEF [United Nations Children's Fund], labeled the world's collective response as "the conspiracy of silence." In late 2003 Stephen Lewis, the UN Secretary-General's special envoy for HIV/AIDS in Africa, expressed grave concerns about the lack of a comprehensive plan for orphans. Fortunately, there are

Jini L. Roby and Stacey A. Shaw, "The African Orphan Crisis and International Adoption," *Social Work*, July 2006, pp. 199, 202–205, 207. Copyright © 2006 by the National Association of Social Workers, Inc. Reproduced by permission.

emerging signs that the global community is mobilizing. As a significant step, in 2001 the UN General Assembly Special Session made specific commitments to address the orphan issue, leading to the identification of a model for orphan care: strengthening the capacity of families, mobilizing and strengthening community-based responses, ensuring access to essential services, strengthening government's role in protecting the children, and raising awareness. These core points, first articulated by the widely accepted document *Children on the Brink*, are to guide the development of national and international orphan care policies and programs. . . .

Determining the desirability of international adoption— particularly adoption of African children by Americans—is not simple. There are justifiable fears and worries at the threshold of such a discussion, on both sides. . . .

Effects of Slavery

The American slavery that began in the early 1500s and lasted through the Emancipation Proclamation in 1865 has been called one of the most tragic episodes in the history of humankind. The century following emancipation saw rampant social discrimination against African Americans, in many ways embedded in the American social structure. The Civil Rights movement has led to significant improvements in government and private sector policies, but studies show that discrimination lingers in subtle ways in health care, higher education, employment, residence, and social status.

In contrast, there are hopeful signs that racial relationships are improving over time. After a review of policies and attitudes between 1940 and 1978, [social psychologists Jack] Dovidio and [Sam] Gaertner suggested that the United States had become more liberal and egalitarian by the late 1970s, noting that changes in mass-media stereotyping had increased race awareness. This positive trend continued into the late 1990s, when [scholars Lawrence] Bobo and [James] Kluegel documented a decline in racial prejudice during the preceding three decades, although government policies intending to bring equality were met with mixed emotions. Other researchers confirmed that attitudes have continuously improved regarding principles of equal treatment, although views regarding government implementation of equal treatment politics and complete integration of neighborhoods and schools are improving at a slower rate.

Slavery was officially banned in Africa in the 1880s, but children there continue to be sold into domestic, agricultural, and sex industries today. An incident in 2001 involving a ship carrying 250 children from Benin and Togo destined for slave labor in Cameroon highlighted this reality in Africa. Rumors that some children may be taken for adoption heightened fears, although there are no documented cases of adoption trafficking into the United States from Africa. Isolated cases of ethical and legal problems in the adoption of children into the United States raise the need for tightened regulations and enforcement of existing federal and state regulations. . . .

Children's Identity and Well-Being

Many have commented on the importance of racial and cultural identity for children in their adoption experience. Thus, transracial adoptions have been opposed by some child advocates in the United States. In the early 1970s, the National Association of Black Social Workers (NABSW) strongly opposed placing African American children in white homes, and transracial adoption subsequently declined. The NABSW has since accepted transracial adoption as an alternative, but in-race adoptions are still viewed as preferable. On this point, the National Association of Social Workers (NASW) has emphasized the need to keep race as an important factor in the adoption matching. The summary of NASW's policy statement on adoption and foster care states, "the placement of choice should be within the child's family. If no relatives are available, every effort should be made to place a child in a home with foster parents of a similar racial and ethnic background to the child's family".

International conventions also recognize the need for cultural continuity. The United Nations Convention on the Rights of the Child (CRC) stressed international adoption as an alternative, "if the child cannot be placed in foster or an adoptive family in the child's country of origin." In addition, the Hague Convention on the Protection of Children and Co-operation in Respect of Intercountry Adoption (1993, hereinafter "the Hague Convention") requires member nations to give priority to in-country placement before considering international adoption. Specific to this article, the question is to what degree African children adopted into the United States would be fostered in their cultural identity, receive acceptance, and enjoy a sense of belonging in their families. Owing to the recency of adopting African children, we were unable to find research data on African adoptees. Hence, we present the next most relevant research: transracial adoption within the United States, specifically white parents adopting African American children, which affords a large body of research data.

[Some studies have reported that transracial adoptees overall are comfortable with their racial identity and that their parents want them to be proud of their racial background.

Some studies show that transracial adoptions may result in negative self-esteem and adjustment outcomes. [Family psychologist Karen] DeBerry and colleagues found that as older children, African American adoptees displayed competence in a Eurocentric orientation, with 40 percent to 60 percent showing maladjustment despite their academic competence. [Adoption scholar Leslie] Hollingsworth analyzed 93 media reports of interviews with transracial adoptees aged 20 and older and found that 82 percent have had difficulty with ethnic identity development, and 97 percent have encountered racism. Other researchers point to racial identity confusion and advocate for policies that encourage same-race placements.

Others have reported that transracial adoptees overall are comfortable with their racial identity, and that their parents want them to be proud of their racial background. [Adoption specialist Karen] Vroegh found that 88 percent of transracial adopted children consider themselves as black or mixed race. Researchers also found that transracial adoptees have secure ethnoracial identities, satisfying adoption experiences, and normal self-esteem levels. Their adjustment is comparable to other adopted children, with 70 percent of placements having satisfactory outcomes. Most people in the United States seem to approve of transracial adoption, but the need to educate families about the importance of the child's racial identity continues.

Children in the U.S. Foster Care System

One of the most sensitive aspects of discussing adoption of African children is the number of children in the U.S. child welfare system, especially the disproportionate numbers of African American children. In September 2001 there were 542,000 children in the U.S. foster care system. Of these, 126,000 children (23 percent) were awaiting adoption (their parents' rights had already been terminated or their permanency goals were set as adoption by state child welfare workers). Of the "waiting" children, 45 percent (56.306) were non-Hispanic African American children. During that year, 50,000 children of all races were adopted from the public welfare system, assisted by incentives given to states and tax credits to adoptive parents, and one-third (17,606, 35 percent) of them were African American. Besides the incentives for adoptive parents, transracial adoptions have also increased as a result of other federal efforts, including the Multiethnic Placement Act, passed in 1994, and the Removal of Barriers to Interethnic Adoption Act, which prohibit race from being a primary factor in public adoptions. Furthermore, the Adoption and Safe Families Act of 1997 and the Adoption Promotion Act of 2003 have increased incentives to adopt more children out of foster care. Still, it is daunting that 126,000 children are waiting for permanent families, and 55,000 to 60,000 of those are African American children.

The number of waiting U.S. children may seem ironic juxtaposed to the increasing number of children being adopted from foreign countries. In 2005 more than 22,300 children were adopted from outside the United States, with the top five countries of origin being Mainland China (7,906), Russia (4,639), Guatemala (3,783), South Korea (1,630), and Ukraine (821). These numbers represent a steady rise over the past 10 years. Why, then, should we discuss adopting African orphans? Arguably, adoption efforts should be focused solely on U.S. waiting children and on culturally appropriate practices for African American children, such as preventive strategies and screening more same-race adoptive families "in" rather than "out."

An increase in international adoptions does not necessarily decrease domestic public adoptions.

However, there may still be some plausible justifications for considering adoption of African children. First, the numbers of children adopted from U.S. public child welfare system and from foreign countries are both on the rise. A five-year (1997 to 2002) comparison of domestic public adoption and international adoptions shows that although international adoptions increased 58 percent, domestic adoptions of children in foster care rose by 64 percent during the same period. During the 2002–2004 period, the domestic rate decreased slightly (3.7 percent) while international adoptions increased by 13 percent. The 2002–2004 figures may indicate a new trend, but could also be a slight variation on the overall pattern.

Although domestic adoption seems to have reached a plateau in 2002 and has since declined slightly while international adoptions have continued to rise, the new federal laws encouraging adoptions should produce another spurt in the rate of adopting U.S. waiting children. It may therefore be fair to speculate that an increase in international adoptions does not necessarily decrease domestic public adoptions. However, this topic needs to be researched more extensively.

There seems to be a growing interest in adopting these children from Africa.

Some Americans may adopt internationally for reasons different from those adopting from the U.S. public system. Some parents may adopt internationally because they are more open to working with private (rather than public) agencies. They may feel apprehension about children who become available for adoption as a result of abuse, neglect, or substance abuse by birth parents. The adoptive families may perceive that international adoptions offer advantages over domestic adoptions, such as ease of approval. In addition, although it is not our intent to promote a practice or policy of "locking out" birth families, some adoptive families may prefer to avoid the now-common practice of open adoptions. Most adoptive parents prefer to adopt children of the same race, but some parents seem to take pride in building a culturally diverse family. Finally, and perhaps most significantly, Americans may view the African situation as an international humanitarian crisis. As in the wake of the Korean conflict, the fall of Saigon, and the demise of communism in Eastern Europe, U.S. families may be drawn to rescue children from an extreme crisis compared with children in the U.S. foster care system, who at least have minimal guarantees of health care, nutrition, and protection. Already, there seems to be a growing interest in adopting these children from Africa.

African Response

The African response to international adoptions has not been adequately explored. It is generally perceived that most African countries do not wish to participate in international adoptions. As previously discussed, in some countries adoption is met with resistance because of cultural beliefs and traditions. Only a handful of African countries are participating in international adoptions into the United States. The highest number of African children were adopted in 2005 from Ethiopia (441, up from 105 in 2002), where the government has approved four U.S. agencies to conduct adoptions. South Africa, Kenya, and Liberia have allowed a few more children to be adopted, but most African nations remain closed to international adoption. Many African countries have lengthy processes that make it difficult to adopt, and some do not allow adoption at all. For example, membership in the Moslem faith is required to adopt in Morocco, complicated laws differ in many states of Nigeria, and adoption is considered only after 18 months of fostering a child in Malawi.

However, international adoption is a legitimate option in the wider context of the orphan crisis. In addition, the African response cannot be generalized, as it appears to vary widely even within one country. On the first author's 2003 trip to Africa, many government and private-sector leaders expressed an interest in exploring the option of international adoptions. Some asked extensive questions about the adjustment of African American children in the United States, the legal and procedural safeguards in the international process, and the rights extended to adopted children. . . .

Part of the Answer

Certainly, the primary solution to the African orphan crisis is to build sustainable, community-based programs to care for the children. Many examples are beginning to spring up, and although the efficacy of such programs in terms of providing for the physical and emotional needs of children should be evaluated, the programs provide culturally appropriate options for children. In-country adoptions should be fostered through education and support. In this larger context, international adoption is not a panacea for African orphans. On the contrary, it is a relatively short-term, small solution to a huge problem calling for efforts on a heroic scale. Only when kinship and community efforts fail to provide a safe and loving family for the child should adoption be considered, starting with in-country options if they are appropriate in the cultural context. In the meantime, the global community should consider the option of international adoption. Adoption must be approached with careful planning and safeguards in place. The numbers of children thus served will be relatively few; but the positive effect on each child may outweigh the potential downsides of international adoption. If carried out with respect to the history and culture of the child's African origins and with meticulous attention to the ethical and legal details, it is possible to offer the gift of a family, safety, and love to a small number of children. In January 2004, UNICEF released an important position statement:

> Inter-country adoption is one of a range of care options which may be open to children, and for individual children who cannot be placed in a permanent family setting in their countries of origin, it may indeed be the best solution.

UNICEF cautioned that the best interests of the child must always be the guiding principle in international adoptions and that the process must provide secure regulations to avoid the risks involved. Although all of the concerns regarding international adoptions cannot be eliminated, there are substantial legal and procedural protections in the United States, and reciprocal protections can be developed bilaterally on the basis of best practice concepts provided in the CRC and the Hague Convention. Toward this end, dialogue should occur between governments, practitioners, and advocates, in both sending and receiving countries.

Adopting Children from China Can Be Fraught with Corruption

Anita M. Andrew

Anita M. Andrew is an assistant professor of history at Northeastern Illinois University.

The year 2007 marks the nineteenth anniversary of a very fragile but enduring diplomatic and immigration arrangement which has permitted American singles and couples to adopt children from China. Adoption statistics for the fiscal years 1988–2004 list a total of 47,501 U.S. immigrant visas issued to Chinese "orphans."

The Chinese children who have been adopted by American citizens since 1988 include mostly infant or toddler girls and some boys with various types of birth defects. They became available for foreign adoption as the result of the population control efforts in place since the early 1980s, known as the "One Child" policy. Rural families emphasized to their sons and daughters-in-law their responsibility to produce at least one son to carry on the family name because of a traditional notion that a son could contribute to the family's income and then care for parents in old age. Most families welcomed one daughter, but a second daughter was often abandoned.

American adoptive parents have long considered China's loss to be their gain. China offered single parents and older parents a unique opportunity that was not usually available in domestic adoptions. They were also drawn to China because they sincerely believed they were saving a child's life.

Anita M. Andrew, "China's Abandoned Children and Transnational Adoption," *Journal of Women's History*, vol. 19, 2007, pp. 123–131. Copyright © 2007 *Journal of Women's History*. Reproduced by permission.

Parents have readily accepted the terms the Chinese government set for these adoptions, including the requirement of travel to China, approximately two weeks in China to complete the adoption process, a cash donation to the orphanage, and promises to the Chinese government about providing for the welfare of the child. As costly and inconvenient as the trip to China is for most American adoptive parents, two main factors make China a desirable choice: the adoptions are finalized in China, providing parents with the peace of mind that comes from finalizing the adoption with both governments before the new family leaves China; and there is never an issue of dealing with a birth parent since all the children available for adoption by foreigners are officially classified by China as "abandoned."

In China, too, baby-trafficking rings are present and are not just a recent phenomenon.

There have been numerous accounts in the Western media since 2001 about how adoptions of children from the other Asian countries, particularly Cambodia and Vietnam, have often been plagued by corruption involving adoption officials in the countries. Americans flocked to China for transnational adoptions in even greater numbers precisely because they regarded it as a safe choice, due to the steps the Chinese government took to ensure that each child was indeed legally available for adoption. A statement is included in the paperwork provided to adoptive parents stating when and where the child was abandoned and that the orphanage worked with police officials to try to determine the abandoned child's parents. There was no reason to question the Chinese government's conclusions or methods until quite recently. There is now mounting evidence, however, that in China, too, baby-trafficking rings are present and are not just a recent phenomenon. . . .

Children Classified as "Orphans"

Every aspect of the transnational adoption process with China since 1988 has hinged on the assumption that the children placed in American homes were abandoned even though adoption agencies routinely use the term "orphan" to describe the children. Prospective parents immediately understand these terms to mean that that the children have become wards of the Chinese state and there is no possibility that a birth parent could appear at the last minute to challenge the adoption.

U.S. international adoption law classifies children adopted from foreign countries as "orphans" if they have no parents or immediate family to care for them. The U.S. Immigration and Nationality Act (originally promulgated in 1952 with subsequent revisions) stipulates that a child brought to the United States by adoption from abroad must meet one or more of the following conditions: "Under U.S. Immigration and Nationality Act (INA), the definition of *orphan* is broader than the common definition. A foreign child may be considered an orphan for the purposes of U.S. immigration law if the child's parents have died or disappeared; if the parents have unconditionally abandoned or deserted the child; or if the child is separated or lost from them. Abandonment normally involves permanent placement of the child in an orphanage."

American parents contract with provincial Chinese orphanages through their adoption agencies to adopt a child. One of the documents supplied to adoptive parents is a statement concerning the child's "abandonment," including information about when and where the child was abandoned. Each orphanage director must also attest to the fact that orphanage personnel together with local police officials conducted a search for the child's parents but no one came forward. There is no way to tell, however, how extensive the process was, or if it was done at all. . . .

No Warning

The testimony of Arthur E. Dewy, Assistant Secretary [of State] for Population, Refugees, and Migration, before the House of Representatives' International Relations Committee, on 14 December 2004 dealt with the [George W.] Bush administration's diplomatic efforts surrounding the "One Child" policy. This statement addressed such practices as involuntary abortions and sterilizations as well as the possibility of the resumption of U.S. funding to the UN Population Fund. Yet there was no mention in this or other Congressional testimony on baby trafficking, although Mr. Dewy and other government officials must have been aware of the news items in the English-language press that year about the problem in China and China's efforts to stop it.

Even more curious is the failure of the U.S. State Department's "Trafficking in Persons Report," of June 2005 to mention the problem. This report included China on the "watch list" with respect to "forced labor and sexual exploitation" but did not mention "baby trafficking" specifically. Moreover, both the Chinese party media and the Western media publicized the cases of baby trafficking, but the Department of State Web site on international adoption continues to omit this information.

There is . . . no way of knowing what will be done with [the adoption] donation or any way to prevent corruption in the system.

There is also a very different tone to the State Department briefing for parents who plan to adopt a child from China. Prospective parents are cautioned about their actions in China and urged to be sensitive to differences in culture. No such tone appears on the briefing sites for adoptions from Cambodia and Vietnam.

Although the State Department's statement on adoption from China does not offer any warnings about their adoption policies, there is one hint in the site briefing that U.S. authorities are aware of the way adoption transactions are made in China, including dealing with orphanage officials in hotels rather than the orphanages themselves and especially the requirement of having to carry large amounts of U.S. currency ($3,000–$4,000) for their donations to the orphanage. The State Department makes a clear effort to defend the donation by stressing that "This 'donation' is *NOT* a bribe, but is required for the adoption and completion of contract for the institute." There is, however, no way of knowing what will be done with this donation or any way to prevent corruption in the system.

All foreign parents who adopt children from China receive detailed instructions from the adoption agency prior to the actual adoption trip instructing them to pay the donation to the child's orphanage in China as part of the fee structure. Yet few adoptive parents are told by their agencies that the amount of money required for foreign adoption donations is astronomically high compared to that paid by Chinese citizens who adopt Chinese children. Foreigners are quite used to being charged a dramatically higher price for everything in China simply because they are foreigners but all other foreigner transactions are acknowledged as financial transactions. Adoptions are not.

The Big Business of China Adoptions

The number of U.S. agencies has mushroomed since the early 1990s from only a handful to well over one hundred in 2005. With an average price ranging between $12,000 to $20,000 to adopt a child from China, not including airfare and hotel accommodations in China, many U.S. agencies look to their China-based programs as the most important services offered clients. The recent adoption credit for transnational adoption covers up to $10,390 of adoption-related expenses. The federal tax credit will help many parents defray most of the cost of such adoptions, yet it is not clear how it will affect the cost of transnational adoptions in the future.

One problem with the success of transnational adoptions from China is that American adoption agencies do not present themselves as businesses but rather as private humanitarian groups that aid both the Chinese children and American clients. Even agencies that are considered nonprofits operate with large staffs of paid case workers, translators, adoption lawyers, and administrators. The high volume of U.S. adoptions from China generates money to pay for those positions.

Another problem involves the disturbing lack of oversight over the adoption agencies and their policies. Information on fees, staff credentials, and parent complaints is not methodically compiled and published to provide state licensing agencies, judicial officials, prospective parents, and academic researchers easy access to the information in order to evaluate every adoption agency that handles adoptions from China.

Another problem involves the disturbing lack of oversight over the adoption agencies and their policies.

Finally, there is the issue of how to assess the credentials of case workers who are involved in placements from China. Adoptive parents deserve to have the best qualified and most dedicated agencies working with them and the children placed from China. It is difficult to tell one adoption agency from another. They all pitch their services in glossy brochures and well-designed Web sites. Most adoption agencies do list the social work backgrounds of their employees, but I know of no agency that requires its case workers to have an academic training in Chinese language and area studies, familiarity with current Chinese politics and society, and so forth.

More Disclosure Is Needed

The current stage of America's adoption relations with China has many problems that have not been adequately addressed either by the U.S. government, which oversees the adoption, or by the adoption agencies, which contract with American parents. Parents who adopt children from China should be provided with a comprehensive briefing about current political and societal conditions that could potentially affect the outcome of the adoption. Unfortunately, this information is not readily available to adoptive parents at the present time.

Parents thus have instead learned to turn to such organizations as Families with Children from China (FCC) for almost all China-based adoption information; the FCC helps parents help each other through regional chapters and online chat rooms. FCC is a very well-intentioned and dedicated parent organization. It does much to provide moral support and information about how to negotiate through the sometimes very long adoption process. It does not have any professional expertise about China, however. The vast amount of and type of information it presents on its Web site must seem overwhelming to most parents.

One way to offer a more manageable and reliable sort of guidance to parents on topics of Chinese history, politics, language, and culture would be to establish an official link between such parent organizations as FCC and such professional organizations as the Asia Society, the Association of Asian Studies, and The Association of Asian American Studies. Parents and their children would have greater access to information about China though academic specialists. Researchers would have an opportunity to create a new field of academic studies related to transnational adoption from China, and the experiences of Chinese-American adopted children. Still, the most serious continuing problem affecting transnational adoptions from China throughout its history concerns the fact that there have not been enough advocates to speak up for the rights of the parents and the children despite the ratification of the Hague Convention on Protection of Children and Cooperation in Respect of Intercountry Adoption.

The current stage of America's adoption relations with China has many problems that have not been adequately addressed.

The recent disclosure in the media of Chinese efforts to curb the black market in babies may have some effect on the type and amount of information and support provided to parents and children who adopt a child from China. Yet I doubt that the U.S. government will take an aggressive stance on issues related to transnational adoption. In all likelihood, transnational adoption policy will continue to follow the lead of foreign policy and trade policy, with the main objective being to engage China's cooperation. As an economic and nuclear superpower, China carries a lot of clout and it does not respond well to interference from foreigners in domestic matters. Yet the issue of China's abandoned children is not simply a domestic concern. If China's adoption system continues to show signs of distress and corruption, the United States may someday have to decide if it is willing to initiate the same warnings and sanctions for China as it has imposed on Vietnam and Cambodia. In 2005, the United States does not seem to be willing to risk its relationship with China to take such a strong stand; it is unclear if that would change in the near future.

Moreover, unless adoption agencies begin to provide full disclosure on each and every Chinese child placed, including information supplied by police authorities about the abandonment, parents cannot be absolutely sure that a child from China was abandoned by a birthparent rather than stolen or sold. Under the present system, there are few guarantees. Nonetheless, if agencies are unable or unwilling to provide such an assurance, how can they legitimately argue that they are truly acting in the best interest of the children they place?

Should Adoptive and Birth Families Be Allowed Contact with Each Other?

Chapter Preface

According to the National Center for Health Statistics, 1.5 million children were born to unwed parents in 2004. Of these children, many are put up for adoption. Putative fathers, named or presumed fathers, are often given few rights in these cases. Although the U.S. Supreme Court has granted parental rights to these fathers if paternity can be proven, the Court has issued no direction as to how those rights should be honored. Therefore, each state is charged with determining the best way to ensure putative fathers are notified about the pending adoption of their children. Given the wide range of laws in each state, the potential for having those rights violated is high; however, some birth mothers contend it is their right alone to determine whether their children should be placed for adoption.

Twenty-three states have established putative-father registries. Presumed fathers can acknowledge their claims to paternity with the registries, which are maintained by state-run agencies. In most cases, registered fathers are notified if legal actions are taken to put their children up for adoption or to terminate parental rights. According to Adoption Under One Roof, a Web site devoted to helping visitors understand adoption laws in Georgia, one of the main reasons to support putative father registries is that "the vast majority of birth fathers refused to sign relinquishment papers, even when they had no intention of parenting the child. The result was that most infant adoptions were considered 'at risk' because the birth father could choose to parent at any time up until the adoption was finalized in court." Obviously, these delays concern adoptive parents, possibly leading them to choose children whose paternity had been legally verified and surrendered.

However, these registries have recently come under fire because some putative fathers have alleged that for-profit adoption agencies use them unfairly and that they only serve to punish men for having nonmarital sex. In most states, if a man does not register with the state, then he has no rights to the children he may have fathered. According to an article by John Cote in the *South Florida Sun-Sentinel,* "The law doesn't require unwed fathers be notified their children are up for adoption unless they are registered—even if the adoption agency knows the father's whereabouts." This practice can lead to some adoption agencies rushing to finalize at-risk adoptions before the father is even aware his parental rights are about to be terminated. Cote discovered that few men in Florida know about the registry, citing the low number of registrants (eighty-nine in 2005) versus the high number of children born out of wedlock (ninety-seven thousand).

Although there seems to be no way of ensuring a putative father's rights, Mike McCormick and Glenn Sacks, regular contributors to www.newswithviews.com, argue that "the law should instead require that an honest, exhaustive search for the father be conducted before an adoption can proceed." As the authors in this chapter debate, the role birth parents play in the lives of children who are put up for adoption is complicated. The situation becomes even more difficult when the question of paternity is involved.

Open Adoption Leads to Closeness Between Both Families

Michael Winerip

Michael Winerip has authored many children's books and is a Pulitzer Prize–winning staff writer for The New York Times, *from which the following viewpoint is excerpted.*

In 2001, when she got pregnant, Moriah Dailer was 19, unmarried and a college dropout working as a waitress in Wheeling [West Virginia]. She considered abortion, but didn't have the money, and her parents wouldn't pay. "They weren't anti-abortion," she said. "It was more, 'You planted your garden, you have to live in it.'"

She and the baby's father, Camren Weigand, 20, talked about marrying, but it didn't seem like a great idea. "We were spending the nine months together," she said, "but we weren't necessarily boyfriend and girlfriend. We were not in a good place to raise a child properly. He blamed me for selfishly wanting to give the baby away and keep on partying. But that's not what it was about. I wanted to make sure I didn't screw up another kid."

Two years earlier, Mr. Weigand fathered a child with another young woman, and the State of Indiana had taken custody of that baby. "It was a terrible feeling of guilt, having it happen a second time," Mr. Weigand said.

Ms. Dailer researched adoption online and interviewed four couples. "None clicked," she said. "Our conversations were awkward and choppy and didn't flow." She wanted an open adoption—in which contact between birth parents and child continues after an adoption is finalized—but these couples didn't view it as she did. "They said they'd send pictures once or twice a year and the baby would know my name, but me and the child wouldn't have a relationship. I wanted to be a part of its life though I wasn't in a good place to raise it."

Finding the Right Couple

Then her older sister passed on a letter from a New Jersey couple looking to adopt. Liane Thatcher and Kerry Keane had been married seven years and were in their 40s. He was a violin maker and works for Christie's auction house as its senior musical instrument specialist; she had a graduate degree and manages an artist's studio. The letter described their interests—music, reading, canoeing, fly fishing, birding. And their quirks: She's a vegetarian; he's a duck hunter. It was decorated with 10 pictures of them with their nieces and nephews.

They printed 400 copies and asked people to pass them on. A friend Mr. Keane hadn't seen in 20 years gave it to a fellow birder in West Virginia, who turned out to be the older sister of Moriah Dailer.

"It was very thoughtfully written," Ms. Dailer said. "And I liked the pictures around the border." Camren Weigand was not so sure about the couple in the photographs. "They looked a little old to me," he said. But they hit it off from the first phone call. The New Jersey couple wanted an open adoption. "We believe secrecy in life is not a good thing," Ms. Thatcher said. "This should be about what's best for the child, and we think it's important that children know where they come from historically and genetically."

While there are no national statistics, open adoption is increasingly common, according to Harold Grolevant, a University of Minnesota professor who is one of the leading experts in the field. He's been doing research with 35 adoption agencies for the last two decades and says there has been a clear-cut swing from confidential to open adoptions. Susan Caughman, editor of *Adoptive Families* magazine, started an Ask the Experts column [in 2007] on open adoption, which, she says, now gets more queries than any other column at the magazine.

When it was time for Ms. Dailer to give birth, the baby's father as well as the adoptive parents were there in the delivery room. The adoptive parents selected a half-dozen names then let the birth parents make the final choice. Phelan Daniel Thatcher-Keane, 7 pounds, 9 ounces, was born Sept. 29, 2001. The adoptive parents were free to leave West Virginia within a few days, but stayed a week and a half. "We sat around and told stories and got to know each other," Ms. Dailer said.

[Some adoptive parents] believe by being open, they will avoid problems that can come when grown children go hunting their birth parents.

An Ongoing Relationship

Since then, the birth parents, their parents and friends have visited Phelan a dozen times. Their level of contact is not typical. More common, said Ms. Caughman, is an exchange of letters and photographs.

On one visit to South Orange [New Jersey], six of Phelan's relatives and their friends stayed at the Thatcher-Keane home: the birth mother, birth mother's dad, birth mother's fiancé, fiancé's mother, and two of the birth mother's and fiancé's college friends. They know it sounds strange to outsiders, they know it might not work if people get too territorial or possessive, but it has worked for them. They believe by being open, they will avoid problems that can come when grown children go hunting their birth parents.

"It's worked because we've all determined to do what's best for Phelan," Ms. Thatcher said. "You gradually get to like each other and trust each other. Moriah's never crossed an inappropriate boundary by trying to correct our parenting." Each visit, she's thanked them for the job they're doing with Phelan.

While it's hard for outsiders to keep everyone straight, Phelan, now 6, seems to have a firm grasp on what's going on. Looking at pictures with a visitor, he says: "That's Moriah. She's my birth mother. Camren, he's my birth father. And that's me with Mom and Dad. And that's Granny Carmen"— his birth father's mother. For Phelan, it's meant more cousins and grandparents to play with.

Despite the openness, giving up a child still tore at the birth parents. Ms. Dailer went through therapy and says it took two years before she stopped feeling like she was 60. She returned to Berea College in Kentucky to finish her degree and sometimes heard harsh comments from younger students. "No. 1, 'How could you give up your baby?' No. 2, 'What makes you think you're not screwing up by letting him know he has two moms and two dads?'"

In 2004 she began a serious romantic relationship; in 2005, Phelan was with her on stage when she got her Berea diploma; in 2007, he was the ring bearer when she married. She and her husband, Ben Kahn, live in Washington State, where she works painting and varnishing boats.

Despite the openness, giving up a child still tore at the birth parents.

Mr. Weigand, the birth father, continues to move around, working now as a farm laborer in Hawaii. "It took six to eight months to stop feeling sorry for myself," he said. "My dad hasn't talked to me since the adoption."

But he says: "I really grew to love Kerry and Liane. It was like an aunt and uncle I never had. And Phelan's not gone. He has a bigger family; he's got love coming from everywhere. He's got a great life—a lot's going on in New Jersey."

Nor does the story end there. [In 2007], Mr. Weigand's sister, Sarah Brewer, of Clayton, [Indiana,] unexpectedly became pregnant. She is 29, has four children ages 2 to 11, is in the midst of a divorce and is going back to school to become a medical assistant. As Phelan's aunt, she knew about his open adoption. At family gatherings, she'd met Ms. Thatcher and Mr. Keane.

On Dec. 1, 2007 in Danville, [Indiana,] Mrs. Brewer gave birth to a 7 pound, 5 ounce girl and handed her over to Ms. Thatcher and Mr. Keane for adoption: Tallulah Maria Thatcher-Keane. On paper it keeps getting more complicated. Phelan and Tallulah are brother and sister, as well as cousins. But in person, it just seems like family. Within a few days, papers were signed, but the New Jersey family did not go home. They hung around another week and a half, and everyone had time to tell their stories and get to know one another.

Closed Adoption Can Sow Bitterness and Discontent

Marcy Axness

Marcy Axness is a national lecturer on adoption and other parenting issues.

Baby Jessica, Baby Richard . . . Haunting specters of what can go so wrong in an institution that purports to champion children, not turn them into the chattel of Dickensian days. . . .

On a spring day in 1995 the nation watched as four-year-old Danny Warburton (alias Baby Richard) was pried from his parents' arms to go and live with his birth parents. It was a heartbreaking reprise of a scene from the summer of '93, the climax of the most famous adoption custody case ever. . . .

A Child Sacrificed, a Nation Confused

I'm sure none of us will soon forget the tragic story of Baby Jessica, the moral of which was eloquently summed up not by the rhetoric of the attorneys, not by the televised appeals by the Schmidts or DeBoers, but by thirty seconds of footage of a sobbing little girl being pried from her home and parents, screaming as her world was ripped apart—once again—in this pathetic human tug-of-war.

The ordeal of Jessica and the Schmidts and DeBoers left us reeling—frustrated, sorrowful, angry, outraged. But I would venture that for many, the most passionate, gnawing response to this story is "God, what if that happens to us?? What if it happens to our children, our friends?" There is a sense of powerlessness. "What can we do to keep this from happening

Marcy Axness, "Painful Lessons: What We Must Learn About Open Adoption," QuantumParenting.com, 2008. Copyright © 1998–2008 QUANTUM PARENTING. Marcy Axness Ph.D., 818.366.7310. Reproduced by permission of the author.

in our world?" In this state, we are sitting ducks for those wielding compelling misinformation.

[Baby] Jessica's ordeal illustrates beautifully why open adoption must be fully understood, and practiced correctly and consciously.

Misunderstanding Open Adoption

I was appalled to hear a television news reporter say to the anchorperson, as a post-script to her story on the Jessica outcome, "This is not the norm, these stories are rare, and usually, the names of the adoptive parents are kept secret." Are we going to let the DeBoer/Schmidt tragedy set adoption consciousness back 30 years?? To let this scare us away from open adoption is to misunderstand true open adoption, and indeed, over the many months of intense social conversations on the topic, which sprang up in bank lines and at cocktail parties during the DeBoer debacle, I discovered that most people do not understand what true open adoption is.

But Jessica's ordeal illustrates beautifully why open adoption must be fully understood, and practiced correctly and consciously. Hers was an "independent" or "private" adoption, something that has become very prevalent as prospective adoptive parents aren't willing to endure the endless waiting, scrutiny, and red tape long associated with agency adoptions. These independent adoptions are frequently labeled "open," since there is often fully-identified information exchanged, and indeed, contact between the birth mother (or birth parents) and the prospective adoptive parents.

The opportunity to select the adoptive parents is often what attracts birth parents to this form of adoption. Conversely, many adopting parents merely accept the contact with the birth parents as a necessary—but not necessarily welcomed—part of the adoption process. Many of these so-called "open" adoptions are emotional time-bombs—most never go off as violently as the one we all grimly witnessed, but some do. Indeed, the sad fact is that there are many more cases like Jessica's that we never hear about. And the response of many is to *tsk, tsk* about how scary and dangerous open adoption is. Yes, it can be, if done without proper, conscientious guidance.

Quality Counseling Is Needed

One of the greatest dangers to a child is to attempt an open adoption without good, *disinterested* counseling. That doesn't mean one or two sessions with a social worker for the birth mother, explaining her options and describing the process, highlighting the benefits to her in open adoption of being able to choose the adoptive parents. And it doesn't mean a coaching session for the prospective adoptive parents in techniques to help keep the birthmother from changing her mind.

Quality counseling for the birth mother (or birth parents), includes:

- An exploration of the dizzying gamut of her feelings

- An evolving understanding of what adoption would mean for her, her child, and the parents she chooses for her child

- Help in realizing that while she may make plans beforehand, she will not be in a position to make a fully-informed decision regarding the adoption until *after her baby is born*

- Preparation for the fact that she will naturally experience feelings of loss and grief if she does choose to relinquish her child for adoption, even if the choice is the correct one for her, and *even though she will have contact with her child and her child's parents*

- Understanding ambivalence! Here is one of the land mines of poorly-done open adoption: when an un-

counseled birthmother, with no post-placement counseling, is blindsided by her stormy emotions after the
separation from her baby, a natural thought is, "I made
a mistake. I've got to get my baby back," even if her
decision to relinquish her child was a sound one and a
right one. You see, we as a society aren't good with
ambivalence—we're conditioned to think that if something is right, it feels good, and if it feels bad or is difficult, it must be wrong.

Quality counseling for prospective adoptive parents includes:

- exploring their own profound losses, of infertility or
  the death or miscarriage of a child or children

- examining their reasons for adopting a child

- embarking on an inner journey to confront *the most
  destructive force in adoption*—their own insecurities and
  fears

Unfortunately, many of the professionals in private open
adoption today are not social workers trained about the complex issues of adoption, but rather, attorneys. Some of them
stress the need for good counseling, but I know for a fact that
many actually discourage it, possibly with the mercenary atti-
tude that warning a birthmother about the potential grief and
loss might threaten the placement.

---

*How adoptive parents respond to their fear . . . deter-
mines the integrity of the first layer of foundation upon
which their adoptive experience, especially their relationship with their child, will be built.*

Facing the Fear of Openness

Jim Gritter is the director of the adoption program Catholic
Human Services in Traverse City, Michigan—an agency at the

forefront of open adoption consciousness and practice. He highlights a basic fact: "Every adoption is a foray into terror."

How adoptive parents respond to their fear—whether they capitulate to it, taking refuge in secrecy and denial, or face it head on and emerge stronger—determines the integrity of the first layer of foundation upon which their adoptive experience, especially their relationship with their child, will be built.

Children intuitively sense in their parents an emotional posture which dreads those questions, even when they've been told, "You can always ask us any questions you have." Such a climate makes for a superficial, somewhat strained relationship between child and parents, not only in adoptive families, but in any family in which there are unanswered questions and questions that can't be asked.

Re-framing to Achieve Peace of Mind

Gritter considers one of his main tasks to be a re-framing of what he terms "desperate, unchecked self-interest" on the part of prospective adoptive parents. When couples come to him wanting to adopt a baby—"By tomorrow, if possible; sundown today would be even better"—Gritter gently guides them from a *What can we get?* orientation to a *What can we give?* orientation. They emerge as a resource for a prospective birth mother, rather than the other way around, and, paradoxically, these couples end up feeling more enriched within themselves, regardless of the final outcome of the adoption.

Indeed, with the help of Gritter's counseling and insight, and a shared journey with a birth mother or extended birth family, hundreds of prospective adoptive parents have reached the threshold of the delivery room in Traverse City with the peaceful conviction that the woman about to give birth is to be respected as a person, and supported in her decision, regardless of whether she chooses to place her baby with them.

They know that there will be another baby for them if she decides to parent, but that there would be no re-gaining of their self-respect, no re-weaving of their torn code of personal ethics, no shaking off the guilt, if they knew they had somehow coerced, manipulated, or impeded that young woman or couple in their process of a lifelong decision.

"You don't want to set yourself up for that, it isn't worth it no matter how desperate you may be," says Mike Spry, an adoptive parent who squarely faced the heartbreak of returning a 4-day-old baby to a birth father who was suing for custody. Spry has often counseled other prospective adoptive parents to aspire to be able to tell a birth mother, after the birth of her baby, "You do what you feel is best, and we will support you 100%." Spry advises, "You can come out of this process with a full sense of entitlement, if you take that step."

The beauty of this kind of re-framing—which is the hallmark of truly child-centered adoption—is eloquently articulated in the book *The Story of David*, by Dion Howells, in which Howells relates the feelings he and his wife shared immediately after the birth of the child who ultimately became their son by adoption.

> Someone is going to leave this hospital with a broken heart. . . . The worst-case scenario in all this is that someone is going to take this little guy home and love him with all their heart. So there is no worst-case scenario for this baby.

Adoptive parents who follow guidelines like these are not saints, or without their everyday hang-ups—in other words, they are no more "cut out" for this type of values-based open adoption than is anyone reading this article. What they have that perhaps others don't is enlightened, experienced guidance.

How Much Contact?

It has become customary in open adoptions for the prospective adoptive parents to develop a relationship with the woman who is carrying the child who may end up being theirs. Sometimes this relationship becomes quite close, whereby the couple becomes a source of emotional support and nurturance for the pregnant young woman, and is invited by her to be in the delivery room for the birth of the baby. This is an issue over which there are many conflicting opinions and attitudes.

Nancy Verrier, adoptive mother and author of *The Primal Wound,* thinks that such a close relationship between prospective adoptive parents and a pregnant woman can end up being subtly coercive, and strongly believes that adoptive parents should not be in the delivery room. Verrier says, "That mother needs to welcome that baby into the world herself, and, if she needs to say goodbye, say goodbye to that baby herself, without anybody else being there."

Adoption is a relationship borne of a series of personal tragedies out of which blessings can come, but blessings which will remain alloyed with pain, grief and loss.

In the context of an ethically rigorous program like the one in Traverse City—in which there is an alertness on everyone's part regarding the possibilities for even the most subtle coercive influences—I think contact between a woman and the prospective adoptive parents of her child can be positive and beneficial. But the potential for abuse of the relationship between prospective adoptive parents and prospective birth mothers is so high that in the absence of those conscientious safeguards, I prefer that it doesn't become the "norm" for open adoption.

The importance and significance of this reality—and the critical need for all parties in an open adoption to recognize this reality—cannot be overstated: *The prospective birthmother is the child's mother, until such time, after the birth of her baby, she makes a considered decision not to parent.* There is plenty of time after the birth of the baby for a mother to make a more fully-informed choice to pursue adoption for her child, and to then meet some prospective adoptive parents. Clearly, this sequence of events will avert many tragedies like Jessica's.

After the Baby Is Adopted

In many of today's open adoptions facilitated by attorneys, there is virtually no encouragement of an ongoing relationship between the birthmother and the adoptee after the birth of the baby, thereby violating the primary hallmark of true open adoption. How many grown adoptees would have different lives, richer lives, had they received a special gift, a photo, even a single letter from a birth mother telling them the simple, honest story of their beginnings, and most importantly, that their mothers didn't give them away because they were somehow bad? I can tell you—many, many, many! (Even Dear Abby agrees with that.)

Truly open adoptions, of course, involve more than The Letter—as one birth mother called that dauntingly important document that she left for her son to read when he was older. Truly open adoption involves ongoing contact, however occasional, between adoptive and birth families, a practice whose benefit/risk ratio is hotly debated by progressive vs. status quo activists. That so many adults adopted through the closed system champion open adoption speaks volumes.

Healing Attitudes About Adoption

I believe that in the adoption industry as it exists today, adoptive parents are tacitly encouraged to paternalistically view the birth mothers as less endowed economically, educationally, culturally, sometimes even morally, and thus less equipped—and deserving—to parent. The seeds are thereby sown for bitterness and contempt down the line if the birth mother should change her mind about placing her child with them, they who would be able to provide a clearly better environment for the child, for *her* child. Part of the quality counseling that is crucial to a safe and successful adoption is learning about the realities of adoption—that it isn't the romanticized "win-win solution to a three-fold problem" society views it as.

> *Open adoption,* as most people perceive and practice it *is emotionally treacherous in its ignorance of the full landscape of the experience and the understanding needed to negotiate it.*

Adoption is a relationship borne of a series of personal tragedies out of which blessings can come, but blessings which will remain alloyed with pain, grief and loss. Loss is a very real dimension of every adoption, but one which is generally overlooked, or even dismissed as so much hogwash by defenders of the status quo in secretive adoption, who promote talking about adoption using terms that eliminate any reference to anything "negative," such as loss or sadness or disappointment.

Even the most "perfect" adoption carries a weighty emotional legacy:

- The depth of loss that the majority of adoptive parents have suffered

- The lifelong effects of adoption on the child's developing sense of self. (Significant numbers of adoptees suffer from a sense of loss, emptiness and rejection, and contend with lifelong issues of abandonment, low self-esteem, control issues and intimacy problems. Adoptees are significantly over-represented in special schools, residential treatment centers and juvenile hall.)

- The grief and loss carried by birthparents and their families. (There is a disproportionately high rate of secondary infertility among birthmothers.)

Complex issues like these are generally acknowledged among the ranks of adoption workers and clinicians dealing with adoptive families, but have yet to pierce our stolid veil of societal denial.

How Then Shall It Be?

Knowledge is power, ignorance is bliss; those embarking on adoption are free to choose, but obliged to live with the consequences of their choices long after the ink fades on the adoption decree. For an adoption is truly made in the heart and soul; legal documents can't bear up what the human spirit can't leaven.

Open adoption, *as most people perceive and practice it* is emotionally treacherous in its ignorance of the full landscape of the experience and the understanding needed to negotiate it. It's like deciding to sky-dive without learning the intricacies of the chute and its mechanism: it may be thrilling, and it may even work—this time—but if it doesn't, there will be a horrible tragedy.

Privacy in Adoption Is a Human Right

Thomas C. Atwood

Thomas C. Atwood is president and chief executive officer of the National Council For Adoption, a national organization that advocates for best practices in adoption.

The issue of "open records" has been hotly debated for decades and the National Council For Adoption (NCFA) has been active in opposing the unilateral and coercive nature of those proposals. NCFA does not oppose reunions or the exchange of identifying information between mutually consenting parties to adoption. What we oppose is the law empowering one party to adoption to force himself or herself on another.

The views of adopted persons, birthparents, and adoptive parents regarding contact and the release of identifying information vary greatly. Many birthmothers, for example, would welcome contact, but many others who have been promised confidentiality would be deeply upset by it. A small minority of adopted persons feel a strong need and even absolute right to this connection. But most adopted persons, though perhaps curious, do not search, and they exhibit little interest in any other family connection beside their adoptive family. One can empathize, especially an adoptive parent such as the author, with any perspective along the spectrum that a person who was adopted or a birthparent might feel about such contacts or exchanges. But considering the wide-ranging and deeply personal views on adoption openness, a mandatory, one-size-fits-all policy is inappropriate. As elaborated in this brief, the decent, compassionate solution is one based on mutual consent.

Privacy Rights in Adoption

The right to maintain or waive one's privacy in adoption is essential to the human rights and personal dignity of adopted persons, birthparents, and adoptive parents. Adoption policy and practice should not empower one party to adoption to receive identifying information or unilaterally impose contacts without the consent of another party. Birthparents and adult adopted persons who desire to have contact should be able to do so, when *both* agree. Otherwise, both should be able to control the release of their identifying information and whether and when contacts are to occur.

Search and reunion advocacy is commonplace in the media, but views among birthparents, adopted persons, and adoptive parents regarding confidentiality and openness in adoption are actually as diverse and personal as they can be. The only just way to reconcile these varying views is through mutual consent, not unilateral coercion. By eliminating even the option of confidentiality in adoption, "open records" laws harm the institution of adoption and unjustly and unnecessarily disrupt the lives of innocent people involved in adoption. If enacted nationally, they would impose a one-size-fits-all, mandatory-openness policy on all adoptions, past, present, and future, even for the many hundreds of thousands of birthparents who were promised confidentiality.

No other counseling relationship between client and professional service provider is subject to state violation of client privacy. If the state may remove a professionally guaranteed right to confidentiality in adoption, what is to prevent the state from attempting to remove that right in relationships with doctors, lawyers, clergy, and others, as well? Eliminating privacy in adoption resulted in the elimination of infant adoption as a viable social institution in Great Britain. It would be tragic and devastating to the interests of children to see that outcome in America. But the same result would likely occur here if mandatory openness became the law of the land, to the detriment of children, birthparents, and families. The institution of infant adoption has already decreased to startlingly low numbers in the U.S.—22,291 in 2002, as compared with 1,365,966 non-marital live births and 1,313,030 abortions (in 2000). . . .

The right to maintain or waive one's privacy in adoption is essential to the human rights and personal dignity of [all involved].

The Harms of Mandatory Open Records

There are several ways that mandatory openness harms adoption, birthparents, children, and families:

First, mandatory openness violates birthparents' basic human right to privacy. "Open-records" policies completely eliminate birthparents' right to choose a confidential adoption, both retroactively and prospectively. To open records retroactively without the approval of a birthmother who was promised privacy is a particularly egregious violation of trust and common decency. For the typical birthmother, making an adoption plan for her child is a supremely loving act, committed in the best interests of her child. The law should honor birthmothers for this act of love, not punish them by stripping them of their basic human right to privacy.

Under mandatory-openness policies, no future birthmother may choose a confidential adoption, no matter what the circumstances of pregnancy or birth, even in the cases of rape or incest. Consider this true story: One birthmother, who placed a child conceived in rape, in preparing to meet with the adult adopted child, was asked by the child to reunite with the father, too! Fortunately, because her identity had not yet been revealed, in accordance with the guidelines of the mutual consent registry in her state, she was able to withdraw from the situation and decline the reunion. A mandatory-openness policy would not have allowed her to avoid a traumatic and even dangerous situation.

"Open records" policies completely eliminate birthparents' right to choose a confidential adoption.

Policymakers, adoption professionals, and the public should recognize that there are any number of legitimate and understandable reasons that birthparents may desire confidentiality—perhaps the birthparent does not want to upset his or her spouse, family, and friends with a never shared revelation; perhaps the birthparent is psychologically or emotionally unable or unready to handle the stress of renewed contact; perhaps the birthmother may be interested in contact some day, but needs to control the timing; perhaps the birthmother does not want to relive the abusive relationship, rape, or incest that caused the pregnancy, or fears possible contact with the birthfather; or perhaps the birthparent simply believes that the healthiest approach for all parties is not to have an ongoing relationship. It is oppressive to impose a one-size-fits-all, mandatory-openness policy, instead of respecting birthparents' loving discernment and their right to privacy.

All states with consent-based openness policies appropriately make exceptions allowing the release of identifying information to adult adopted persons, or parents of minor adopted persons, at a minimum with a legal determination of "good-cause." Thus, unlike mandatory-openness advocates' demands for unconditional access to identifying information, birthparents are not provided an absolute right to privacy. Nor does NCFA advocate an absolute right. However, with limited exceptions, such as a legal determination of "good cause," as minimally allowed in all states with consent-based openness policies, the birthparent should have the right to control the release of her or his identifying information and whether and when contact is to occur.

Second, mandatory openness increases the number of unwanted, unilaterally imposed contacts between adopted persons and birthparents. Providing adult adopted persons identifying birthparent information without birthparents' knowledge or consent increases the number of unwanted, unilaterally imposed contacts. When such a law is passed in a state, many thousands of birthparents, around the state, country, and world, become vulnerable, especially because very few of them are even aware that their privacy has been eliminated. Even if they are aware of the new law, they are powerless to prevent unwanted contacts or control the timing of them. Unwanted reunions between adult adopted persons and birthparents are often highly disruptive and even traumatic for everyone involved. Even when adopted persons and birthparents mutually consent to contact, their satisfaction with reunions and ongoing relationships is quite unpredictable, despite the rosy scenarios often portrayed in the media.

Mandatory-openness advocates frequently offer a "contact preference form" as an attempt to address concerns about unwanted contacts. However, such forms are only indications of birthparent preferences and have no legally binding effect. They still allow the release of birthparents' identifying information without their consent, which is a violation of privacy in and of itself. And they still leave birthparents vulnerable to unilaterally imposed contacts, and the fear thereof, even if such contacts never occur.

Unwanted reunions between adult adopted persons and birthparents are often highly disruptive.

Another slightly better, but still unsatisfactory compromise that is sometimes offered is the "contact veto," which allows birthparents to take an affirmative step legally prohibiting contact. Of course, most birthparents would be unaware that the law had been changed and that they must exercise their contact veto in order to maintain their privacy. This policy has the principle backwards: Persons should not be required to take an affirmative step to *maintain* their privacy; they should be required to take an affirmative step to *waive* it. Furthermore, this policy still violates privacy by releasing identifying information without consent. And once an unwanted contact is made and birthparents' privacy is violated, what recourse do they really have? How many birthmothers are going to press charges against the child they lovingly placed for adoption?

Third, mandatory openness undermines the strength of the adoptive family. A chief reason adoption has been so successful is that society and law have respected the adoptive family as the child's true and permanent family. Adoption is not "long-term foster care," until the child grows up and can reunite with the "real" family. But by empowering one side to force herself or himself on the other, mandatory openness establishes the state as a reunion advocate, rather than the neutral party it should be. It establishes as the legal norm and the cultural expectation that adopted persons and their birthparents will, and should, "reunite" when the child reaches the age of majority. Such a policy not only promotes emotional and traumatic experiences in families, it sends the corrosive message that adoptive families are somehow inadequate to meet the psychological needs of their adopted members.

This message attacks a very foundation of adoption, that the adoptive family is the child's true and permanent family. Adoptive parenting has provided untold social and familial benefits to children throughout the years. Law and society must continue to respect the adoptive family as the adopted person's true and permanent family, in order for those benefits to continue.

Fourth, mandatory openness reduces the confidential options available to women with unplanned pregnancies and causes some women who would otherwise choose adoption to choose abortion. There are significant numbers of women with unplanned pregnancies, who are concerned about privacy in making their decisions regarding their pregnancies. Clearly, some number of these women, who would otherwise choose adoption, would choose abortion if they could not choose adoption with the assurance of confidentiality. What that number would be is impossible to tell, but what does it need to be? The loss of human potential from even one abortion that would have been an adoption is unknowable. As reported in the statistical section of *Adoption Factbook IV*, the ratio of infant adoptions to abortions in America is already extremely low—only 17 domestic infant adoptions for every 1,000 abortions. As stated by the late Jeremiah Gutman, who was a director of the American Civil Liberties Union (ACLU) and chair of the ACLU's Privacy Committee, a woman facing an unplanned pregnancy, without the confidential adoption option, could maintain her privacy *only* if she had an abortion. Should the law grant a woman with an unplanned pregnancy a right to a confidential abortion, but not to a confidential adoption?

Eliminating privacy in adoption would mean that women with unplanned, out-of-wedlock births . . . would have no choice but to single-parent.

Mandatory-openness advocates point to reductions in abortions in selected states to argue that "open-records" policies actually increase the number of adoptions. This assertion defies common sense. Why would more women choose adoption because confidential adoption has been removed from them as an option? The fact is that abortions have gone down in most states in recent years, whatever their policies on adoption records, and there are far more powerful factors influencing that trend than adoption-openness policies. Unlike the mandatory-openness advocates' argument, our point here is not a "macro-economic" assertion, i.e., that mandatory open records increase the overall number of abortions in a state. Rather, the point is a "micro-economic" observation about the psychology of the decision. Some unknowable number of women with unplanned pregnancies, who care about their privacy, will choose a confidential abortion, when the only other confidential option, adoption, is removed. The mandatory-openness policy's arbitrary limitation of confidential options is unjust to women with unplanned pregnancies who care about privacy, whatever their numbers.

Fifth, mandatory openness reduces the number of adoptions and increases the number of children in foster care. Eliminating privacy in adoption would mean that women with unplanned, out-of-wedlock births, who would only choose adoption if it was confidential, would have no choice but to single-parent. Social science data clearly reveal that the more single parents there are, the more children languish in foster care, with greatly increased costs to the child, family, society, and taxpayer as a result. Forcing women to parent when they are not ready to do so leads to more children in foster care, as evidenced by the large increases in the foster care rolls that have occurred, as the number of infant adoptions dramatically declined over the last 30 years.

Sixth, mandatory openness perpetuates the myth that adopted persons face debilitating identity problems that can only be resolved by knowing and having contact with their biological roots. The erroneous assumption of many mandatory-openness advocates is the false and demeaning notion that in order to be psychologically healthy, adopted persons must fulfill a deep-seated need to have identifying information about, and contact with, their biological parents. The truth is that the vast majority of persons adopted at a young age accepts their adoption readily, and grow up to be successful, happy, stable adults at the same rate as people raised in their biological families. While many adopted persons indicate a curiosity about their biological parents, few profess anything approaching a need for identifying information or contact, and fewer still would favor having an absolute right to impose themselves on birthparents.

Seventh, mandatory openness adds nothing to the adopted person's ability to obtain medical information. State laws already allow for adopted persons to request medical or genetic information from birthparents without sacrificing confidentiality—at a minimum, with a showing of "good cause." NCFA supports the principle that the law should provide an efficient process whereby adult adopted persons, and the parents of minor adopted children, can efficiently request medical information from birthparents. But these requests can be fulfilled confidentially, and it is the common practice to do so. Birthparents, agencies, attorneys, and judges alike willingly facilitate this process. In addition, the increasing availability of genetic testing is making the issue of medical records moot. One can obtain more information about one's genetic predispositions from such tests than from medical histories of biological parents. . . .

State laws already allow for adopted persons to request medical or genetic information from birthparents without sacrificing confidentiality.

The Mutual Consent Registry

NCFA advocates the mutual consent registry as the most equitable policy for handling the issue of openness and privacy in adoption. More than 40 states allow birthparents and adult adopted persons, who desire to exchange identifying information and/or have contact, to register with the state their interest in doing so, in which case the state informs both parties and facilitates the process. By allowing birthparents and adult adopted persons to permit or prohibit the release of their identity, the registries facilitate mutually consensual contact, while enabling the parties to safeguard their privacy, if they so choose. Some states allow birthparents to authorize at the time of placement, as part of the adoption approval process, the release or non-release of their identifying information to the adult adopted child upon request. Such policies respect the principle of mutual consent, so long as the birthparent may change his or her designation at any time.

A "match" in a mutual consent registry occurs when both an adult adopted person and a birthparent register with the state their interest in exchanging identifying information and/or contact. Mandatory-openness advocates often attempt to justify their opposition to mutual consent registries by stating that the low frequency of matches is evidence of the policy's ineffectiveness. But any party to adoption interested in contact learns very quickly of the existence of the registry. If an adopted person or birthparent chooses not to register at that point, the logical explanation is that the party is simply not interested in having contact or sharing identifying information, not that the policy "doesn't work." The policy allows the parties to choose. If they do not choose the way mandatory-openness advocates think they ought, that does not mean there is something wrong with the policy. People who choose not to register should be allowed to maintain their privacy.

Elsewhere in *Adoption Factbook IV*, the preeminent researchers in the study of openness in adoptive placements conclude that a "one-size-fits-all approach" regarding "the desirability and undesirability of fully disclosed or confidential adoptions . . . is not warranted. . . . [T]he development of adoptive identity is quite varied, depending on individuals, families, and aspects of the kinship network. . . . But . . . this variation does not appear to be significantly dependent on level of openness." For this reason, NCFA also supports the application of the mutual consent principle to decisions regarding openness in domestic adoptive placements of infants—that is, mutual consent between birthparents and adoptive parents.

As this brief argues regarding openness in adoption records, mutual consent seems to be the decent and just option for adoptive placements, as well: Let the adoptive parents and birthparents agree to the level of placement openness that seems right to them.

Open Adoption Can Lead to Heartache for Both Families

Sonia Nazario

Sonia Nazario is a Pulitzer Prize–winning journalist who writes for the Los Angeles Times *from which the following viewpoint is excerpted.*

Nearly two-thirds of Americans have encountered adoptions in their families or with friends, according to a recent survey. Kendall Pool, however, was special; she was a pioneer in an edgy experiment that has grown into the phenomenon known as open adoption.

Her birth mother would reenter her life and play a large part in it. Children in fully open adoptions remain close to their birth families. They get frequent visits, usually from their birth mothers. Those visits can be quarterly, monthly—even daily. Some birth mothers and adoptive mothers cheer on their children together at soccer games.

Adoption agencies estimate that 90% of infant adoptions in the United States are open enough for adoptive and birth parents to meet at least once—and a quarter are completely open. In 13 states, including California, recent laws allow courts to enforce open-adoption contracts stipulating types of visits and their frequency.

Forty years ago, closed adoptions were the rule. They saved embarrassment, even shame, sometimes for an unwed mother, other times for an infertile couple. Even in the early 1970s, some unwed mothers were sent away to give birth.

Some pregnant women gave birth blindfolded and with their hands tied, or were drugged into comas so they would neither see nor touch their babies. A "clean break," it was called. Their children had their original birth certificates sealed. Many were never told they were adopted.

Forty years ago, closed adoptions were the rule.

Often, however, something was amiss: These adopted children were different from everyone else in their families. Sometimes they found out the truth: They unearthed their adoption papers. Or Uncle Charlie, drunk, blurted out that they weren't really kin. The children had been living a lie: How could they trust their adoptive parents again? Who were their real parents? Were their birth mothers Hollywood starlets? Sunset Boulevard prostitutes? Fantasy mothers who were perfect and would someday come and get them—or, worse, would not?

Even children who had been told they were adopted knew very little about their birth families.

Why had they been given up in the first place?

Social workers noticed worrisome signs. Adoptees struggled with their identities more than most teenagers. Many had trouble with trust and commitment to good relationships. Among children who had been adopted as infants, had never been in foster care and had grown to school age, 41% had seen a counselor for emotional or behavioral problems, compared with 18% of their non-adopted peers, according to a 2004 study by Illinois State University. And 24% had enrolled in special education classes, compared with 9% of non-adoptees.

Some social workers, notably in California, Wisconsin, Michigan and Texas, said adoption had to open up. Some birth mothers joined their cause.

Others, including the National Council for Adoption, lobbied otherwise. Some adoptive parents joined their cause. They said most adoptees were neither troubled by nor interested in their birth families. Open adoptions, they said, would keep their children from bonding with them and create confusion and divided loyalties. Some foresaw terrible struggles with birth parents. One authority said this could cause emotional child abuse. A growing number of couples went abroad to adopt children, sometimes to keep birth parents an ocean away.

Even children who had been told they were adopted knew very little about their birth families. Why had they been given up in the first place?

A pathfinder through all of this was Kendall Pool, who became a toddler, then a growing child, then a teenager. Today [2007] she is 23 years old. In the annals of open adoption, her experience has been more difficult than most. Because she is a pioneer, her parents did not benefit from experience with open adoption that has developed over the years. Proponents say open adoption generally works.

Is it a good thing? Has it been good for Kendall?

Or bad?

Obstacle After Obstacle

A few hours after Kendall's birth mother left her behind, a couple drove from Los Angeles to Antelope Valley Hospital. David McArthur, 36, was a psycho-physiological researcher at UCLA and the Sepulveda Veterans Administration Hospital. His wife, Dorothea, 40, known as Dorrie, hoped this drive would end a four-year heartache.

Back when she was 35, Dorrie had thought she possessed everything: a good marriage, two master's degrees, a PhD in clinical psychology, her own practice, a Spanish-style home on a hill overlooking Silver Lake and a weekend beach house in Carpinteria [California]. But then one morning, she awoke in a panic. She wanted a baby. For a year, she tried to get pregnant. Finally, a test showed that she couldn't.

A Beverly Hills attorney arranged an adoption, but when the baby was born, the birth mother backed out. Now, driving up the 14 Freeway to the high desert, Dorrie was worried. Her lawyer had found another baby, but there had been only two meetings with Patti Pool, the birth mother. Both meetings were at a Denny's restaurant. Only a few words were spoken about the birth father. He wasn't even there.

When Dorrie and David reached the hospital, they found the new baby waiting. Her shocks of brown hair were tucked under a little pink hat, and her blue eyes peered out of a small white blanket wrapped snugly around her. Overjoyed, the McArthurs took her home. Her name was Kendall. They re-named her Miranda, after a character whose name they liked in Shakespeare's play *The Tempest*.

What if Miranda grew up to love her birth mother more? What if she wanted to someday go live with her?

When Miranda was 3 1/2, Dorrie got a surprise. It was a birth announcement from Patti, forwarded by Dorrie's adoption attorney. In addition to Jed, her half-brother, Miranda now had a half-sister. Her name was Bryhannah.

That same day, by coincidence, Dorrie met with Sharon Roszia, an adoption expert in Orange County, who brought up the possibility of an open adoption. The mother in Dorrie wanted to run from the idea. What if Miranda grew up to love her birth mother more? What if she wanted to someday go live with her?

But the psychologist in Dorrie could not dismiss the proposal. Wasn't Miranda entitled to know her birth mother? Her only sister? Wasn't it cruel to deny a child her past? Inevitably, Miranda would learn she was adopted, and it would make her feel rejected. Openness might help her deal with this central loss.

It might prepare her for any genetic vulnerabilities. And if she could feel loved by both of her families, it might boost her self-esteem. She would know where her strengths came from—and her weaknesses. It might help her figure out her future.

Dorrie and David decided. They would welcome Patti into Miranda's life, with just one understanding: The adoption was final; only the McArthurs would raise her. . . .

Eager as Miranda was to meet her birth mother, the news that she had another mommy scared her. The next afternoon, she awakened from her nap, screaming: The lady who grew her in her tummy had come to snatch her away. On the beach at Carpinteria, she reached a sandy hand for Dorrie's. "You are my only mommy, right?"

Even in Patti's new life, Miranda's adoption made her feel guilty.

Dorrie tried to ease her fear. She hung photo collages showing how long Miranda had been part of the McArthur family. But Dorrie also showed Miranda pictures of her other mommy. The pictures included Bryhannah and Jed. Dorrie listened as Miranda zeroed in on the obvious: Her other mommy had kept two children. But she gave Miranda away. Miranda must have been ugly, a bad baby who cried too much.

No, no, Dorrie said, soothingly.

Like most adoptees, Miranda had another fear: Would her adoptive parents abandon her the way her birth parents had?

She tested her adoptive parents with defiant behavior that created security—and terrible anxiety: If she behaved badly, and if David and Dorrie kept her, then she was safe. But what if she behaved very badly? Very bad behavior was the real test. . . .

A Spate of Tantrums

When Patti received Dorrie's gift box containing the invitation to open Miranda's adoption, she was stunned. Locked away in her closet was another box, a shoe box, stuffed with everything that might remind her of the baby she had left behind.

She had joined the Army, completed her service and moved half a dozen times, finally back to Southern California. Bryhannah had been conceived during a one-day affair with an Army doctor. Now Patti was married to still another man. Even in Patti's new life, Miranda's adoption made her feel guilty. What if she saw Miranda and wanted to grab her and run? What if she didn't want to? Would it mean something was wrong with her?

Would Miranda love her? Hate her?

At Dorrie's urging, Patti consulted with Sharon Roszia, the adoption expert, and finally agreed to come to Miranda's house. She would bring Jed, now 5, and Bryhannah, 4 months.

"I want to see them," Miranda said, "but just once."

They arrived at noon on a clear, sunny day.

Neither family would forget how Miranda, 3 years and 7 months old, climbed into Dorrie's arms and stared hard at Patti. She said nothing.

"Hello, Miranda," her birth mother said.

Nothing.

Bryhannah was at Patti's breast, nursing. Miranda decided to defend Dorrie. She fondled her adoptive mother. "My mommy has breasts too!"

But she wrestled with the ambiguity. "Am I going to stay here with my mommy and daddy?"

"Yes," Patti replied, relieved to see how loved Miranda was. "Forever. This is your home, and they are your mommy and daddy. I will never take you away."

Miranda would remember seeing Patti's pain.

After the visit, Miranda seemed remarkably at ease. She asked Dorrie to pretend to be her sister and play with her. Two days later, she sat on Dorrie's lap. She had a faraway look.

"What are you thinking?" Dorrie asked.

"About Bryhannah and Jed," Miranda replied, wistfully.

She awoke several times that night. "I want to go see where they live and then come home again."

As Miranda grew, she was drawn ever more to her birth family.

But the prospect brought a spate of tantrums. "Are you trying to see if I will give you away if you are very difficult?" Dorrie asked, exasperated.

"Yes!" Miranda said. . . .

Back to Her Birth Name

As Miranda grew, she was drawn ever more to her birth family.

Patti appreciated bright colors. Miranda liked hot pink, purple and orange. Patti was athletic and loved riding a Harley-Davidson. Miranda excelled at gymnastics and was happiest upside down on a monkey bar.

David McArthur, on the other hand, built a harpsichord. He and Dorrie sang in a classical choir. Miranda couldn't carry a note. The shelves in the McArthur home were loaded with learned tomes. Miranda repeated first grade. Tests showed she had a learning disability.

To ease Miranda's adoption anxieties, David and Dorrie sent her to a psychologist. When she was asked to rank the people in her life, Miranda listed birth family first. During Patti's visits, Miranda asked: "Do you love me even when I'm bad?" The answer was always yes. Occasionally, she crawled into Patti's lap, if only for a few seconds. Each visit seemed to decrease Miranda's sense of being rejected.

But the differences between Miranda's two families took a toll. Dorrie and David found Patti self-centered and impulsive. When she joked once about swapping kids, Dorrie bristled. Patti, in turn, found it difficult to trust Dorrie. When Dorrie said she was keeping an adoption journal, Patti, who was chatty, began to measure her words, afraid that Dorrie might write them down and use them against her.

To ease Miranda's adoption anxieties, David and Dorrie sent her to a psychologist.

Patti divorced her second husband after a fight so brutal it prompted a friend to call the police. Now she had to work the graveyard shift as a medical clerk. Sometimes she could not scrape together enough pennies to buy milk for Jed and Bryhannah. Her utilities were cut off. When her monthly food stamps ran out, she took her children to her parents in Lancaster for dinner. Finally, she was evicted, and she moved in with her parents, who by then were living in a double-wide trailer in San Diego County.

Her visits to Miranda grew less frequent.

Miranda, now 6, tried to hold on to her. She learned that Patti's name for her had been Kendall. In a burst of tears, she told Dorrie she wanted to be called Kendall—but that she was afraid to go to court to change her name. "Maybe they will take me away!"

Dorrie hugged her and said she didn't have to go to court.

Miranda learned to spell Kendall and then to write it. She coached her reluctant parents. "Mother?" she said, then directed Dorrie to reply: "Yes, Kendall." After a while, she answered only to Kendall. Even if the house were burning down, she said, she would not respond unless they called her Kendall.

She and her adoptive parents compromised: Miranda-Kendall. But slowly, she became simply Kendall. To Dorrie, the change seemed to make Kendall more affectionate.

With the name change, however, Kendall began having nightmares again. But now they were about Dorrie. In Kendall's dreams, Dorrie was stung by a bee. Dorrie was hospitalized, and she left Kendall alone. Then Dorrie was arrested—and she left Kendall by the side of the road.

Kendall sang a new song she had thought up especially for Dorrie, who would recall its title years later: "You Are the Loveliest Mother." She pulled out a doll that Patti had given her. Kendall had named the doll Baby. She made Baby jump up and down to get Dorrie's attention, and then she questioned Dorrie about adoption.

She asked Dorrie to play hide-and-seek and to call out: "I HAVE to find my daughter! I will not lose my daughter!"

Eventually, Kendall's anxiety eased again. . . .

Unspoken Resentment

Lurking beneath everything, however, were the differences between Kendall's families.

Patti spanked her children, sometimes with a belt. Once, when Jed stole some money, she stripped his room of everything but his bed and dresser and put him in "jail" for a month. He could come out only to go to the bathroom and to school.

Dorrie, on the other hand, believed that parents should never hit children. When Kendall misbehaved, Dorrie took pains to explain why she shouldn't. She coaxed Kendall to say why she was being naughty. She gave her timeouts and stopped her allowance. At worst, Dorrie canceled visits to Kendall's birth family until her behavior improved.

Patti harbored a strong and mostly unspoken resentment about what she saw as Dorrie's leniency. But to Dorrie, her way was important for Kendall, whose adoption and learning difficulties could cause shame and low self-esteem. When Kendall had trouble at school, Dorrie moved her, hoping to find somewhere she would fit. Kendall switched elementary schools three times.

How, Patti wondered, would Kendall ever adjust to life in the real world? Maybe Dorrie was great at tackling other people's problems, but not her own daughter's. Was Dorrie spoiling her to ensure that she loved Dorrie more?

Why, Jed and Bryhannah wondered, couldn't they get away with things the way Kendall could?

When Dorrie canceled visits, Bryhannah took it personally.

Patti feared that reminding Kendall constantly about being adopted increased her insecurity.

So did Patti. It fed her growing resentment that open adoption went only one way. It also seemed to Patti that Dorrie overemphasized the fact that Kendall was adopted. Kendall's first doll, a gift from a friend of Dorrie's, came with adoption papers. Since Kendall was 5, Dorrie had read adoption books to her. Together, they watched adoption programs on TV. Each year, the McArthurs celebrated Kendall's adoption day.

Adoption, Patti thought, should be a place setting on Kendall's table—but not the centerpiece. Patti feared that reminding Kendall constantly about being adopted increased her insecurity.

Patti began to withdraw. Alarmed, Dorrie scheduled both families to attend sessions with Kendall's psychologist. Patti drove home from the first session secretly seething. The whole exercise, it seemed, was designed to persuade her—and only her—to change her behavior. She found each visit with the McArthurs emotionally exhausting.

Patti stopped calling. It was enough that Kendall knew everyone loved her; she would be fine.

When Kendall turned 9, her birth mother missed a birthday visit to Disneyland—and a therapy session. Kendall received a gift from Patti, but it was a week late—and there was no card, not even a note.

Kendall wondered: Had she done something wrong?

She began doing poorly in school. Before each visit to her therapist, she developed a rash. At Thanksgiving that year, she asked Dorrie to not talk about Patti. It made her too sad. . . .

Finally, in June 1993, Kendall called her birth mother, but Patti's telephone was disconnected. Kendall's grandparents knew where Patti was, but they wouldn't tell.

Kendall's birth mother had disappeared.

CHAPTER 4

What Issues Are Involved in Nontraditional Adoptions?

Chapter Preface

It is estimated that thousands of children available for adoption in the United States have special needs. Special needs can range from suffering from chronic physical illnesses such as AIDS or epilepsy to mental illnesses such as attention deficit disorder and Tourette syndrome. The severity of these diseases can range from mild to completely debilitating, and these children are far less likely to be adopted than children who might need less care. Despite the struggles children with special needs and their adoptive parents face, many live happy, healthy lives.

Choosing to adopt a child with special needs must be done with considerable thought given to the challenges ahead for all parties involved. For example, children with severe disabilities may need additional routine care, regular medical attention, and extra help with academics. Potential parents must consider these needs before making the decision to adopt. In addition, adopting a child with special needs can present challenges to the family. Judith Lavin, author of *Special Kids Need Special Parents*, reminds new parents, "Realize that you will need patience, ingenuity and strength to take on the additional challenges. Make sure you have or will have a flexible schedule to accommodate the child's medical needs."

Even children who appear free of physical and mental disabilities can develop problems after they are adopted. Many older children who have been in foster care for many years can develop adjustment problems that can severely hamper their progress in their new environments. In *Adoption in the United States*, Martha Henry and Daniel Pollack caution, "Children adopted from foster care frequently have ongoing problems related to attachment disorder, trauma, abuse and neglect, and behavioral, developmental and psychological disorders." They urge routine screenings and follow-up care to help families adjust.

Nonetheless, there are many success stories of adopted children with special needs and their new families. Teri Bell, a social worker and advocate for international adoptions of children with special needs, has worked with more than a thousand children with special needs in her twenty-five year career. Although some of these adoptions have ended in heartache for all parties involved, "the majority of families, however, feel[s] that the addition of their child with special needs was one of the greatest experiences of their lives." Lessons learned from these children have enhanced their families and made them stronger as individuals.

Rachel Pickett, an advocate for children with special needs, notes, "Special needs children who are not adopted usually end up spending their lives in a hospital ward or home [for children with special needs]." Given that evidence clearly states that children with special needs have a better quality of life when they live in a stable, family-oriented environment, it seems vital that these children are adopted by loving, caring parents who are dedicated to their care. As the authors in this chapter argue, there are as many ways of forming a family as there are members who make up those families.

Adoption by Gay Men and Lesbians Is a Good Option for Orphaned Children

Julian Sanchez

Julian Sanchez is a journalist and contributing editor to Reason *magazine, from which the following viewpoint is excerpted.*

Right now only Florida explicitly prohibits any gay person from adopting, but just six states and the District of Columbia explicitly *allow* adoptions by homosexuals. In most cases there's no formal policy, and several states either are known for family judges disinclined to grant homosexuals custody or have indirect statutory barriers to gay parenting. Nebraska banned gay foster parenting in 1995. Mississippi and Utah allow only married couples to adopt, a restriction geared in both cases to exclude gay couples. Just under half of U.S. states permit "second-parent adoption," which grants parental rights to both members of an unmarried couple, in at least some jurisdictions. And more restrictions may be on the way.

From a civil libertarian perspective, it's clear enough why the unequal treatment of gay parents is objectionable: The human desire for family isn't exclusive to heterosexuals, and attempts to prevent gays from raising families both stigmatize them and threaten to deprive them of an important component of a full life. But these barriers to adoption should also offend anyone concerned about family values—about ensuring that all children, especially those who have suffered in the past, find loving homes, and that enrolling those kids in school or getting them medical care is a simple, routine procedure, not a legalistic obstacle course. Yet "family values" remains the call to arms of many who support restricted parenting.

Julian Sanchez, "All Happy Families, the Looming Battle over Gay Parenting," *Reason*, August/September, 2005. Copyright © 2005 by Reason Foundation, 3415 S. Sepulveda Blvd., Suite 400, Los Angeles, CA 90034, www.reason.com. Reproduced by permission.

In 2004 the U.S. Supreme Court refused to hear an appeal of a lower court decision upholding Florida's ban on gay adoption. The challenge was brought by the American Civil Liberties Union [ACLU]. . . .

Some lawmakers and judges in other states do indeed share a horror of gay parenthood. In 2003, as he introduced a bill to ban gay foster parenting, Texas legislator Robert Talton (R-Pasadena) told the state's House of Representatives: "If it was me I would rather [leave] kids in orphanages as such— this is where they are now if they're not fostered out. At least they have a chance of learning the proper values." (Texas doesn't actually have orphanages, but you get the point.) Talton pushed a similar bill through his state's House in April [2005], though Talton's language was later stripped from the Senate version of the law. Former Alabama Supreme Court Judge Roy Moore used uncommonly vehement language, but perhaps not uncommon logic, when he wrote in 2000 that a lesbian mother should be denied custody of her three children because homosexuality was "an evil disfavored under the law," and that the state should "use its power to prevent the subversion of children toward this lifestyle, to not encourage a criminal lifestyle."

There are at least a quarter million children living in households headed by same-sex couples.

Reasons for Retaliation

State legislatures are now pushing to erect a variety of legal barriers to gay couples seeking to raise kids. Carrie Evans, state legislative lawyer for the Human Rights Campaign, a gay advocacy group, has tracked state legislation on gay parenting since 2000. "This year [2005] has been the worst," says Evans. "Usually we have a few, but I've never seen this many in one year." Just four months into 2005, lawmakers in seven states— Alabama, Arkansas, Indiana, Oregon, Tennessee, Texas, and

Virginia—had introduced bills that would restrict the parenting rights of gay couples and individuals. This new assault seems to be the result of several complementary factors:

The Gay Baby Boom: Extrapolating from 2000 census data, Urban Institute demographer Gary Gates conservatively estimates there are at least a quarter million children living in households headed by same-sex couples; 4.2 percent are either adopted or foster children, almost double the figure for heterosexual couples. (Single gay parents, of course, are not captured by those numbers.) While the increase in gay parenting can't be precisely measured, Gates estimates that one in 20 male same-sex couples and one in five female couples were raising children in 1990. By 2000 those figures had risen to one in five for male couples and one in three for female couples. A 2003 survey by the Evan B. Donaldson Adoption Institute found that 60 percent of adoption agencies place children in gay households, and a 2001 Kaiser Family Foundation survey found that, while about 8 percent of gay respondents were currently parents or guardians of children under 18, almost half of those who weren't hoped to one day adopt children of their own. As the ranks of gay parents swell, they become more visible—and more visible targets.

As the ranks of gay parents swell, they become more visible—and more visible targets.

The Tipping Point: A 2004 Harris poll found that a plurality of Americans still disapproves of adoption by same-sex couples—43 percent and 45 percent for female and male couples, respectively. But that represents a dramatic decrease in opposition since 1996, when majorities of more than 60 percent disapproved in both cases. Conservatives may worry, with good reason, that if laws restricting gay parenting aren't locked in now, perhaps drawing strength from the momentum behind anti–gay marriage legislation, their time will soon have passed.

The Marriage Factor: "Among both the youngest and oldest cohorts," a 2003 study by the Pew Forum on Religion and Public Life found, "those who know someone who is gay are about twice as likely to favor gay marriage as those who do not." The expansion of gay parenting means people who might not otherwise encounter gay couples will be more likely to see them at PTA meetings and Little League games. And the Harris poll found an overwhelming majority agrees that children being raised by gay couples should "have the same rights as all other children." For practical purposes, that means ensuring that their parents have rights too. If, other things being equal, it's better for children to be raised by married couples, then as the number of kids raised by gays increases, the conservative case for expanding marriage rights becomes more potent. All of which means that as more same-sex couples raise children, opposition to gay marriage is likely to erode—a matter of concern to the social conservatives on whom Republican politicians increasingly rely for support.

The *Lawrence* Effect: Until recently, sodomy laws in 13 states confirmed Judge Moore's assessment of homosexuality as "an evil disfavored under the law." But in the 2003 case *Lawrence v. Texas*, the [U.S.] Supreme Court held that sodomy laws were unconstitutional, yielding, in the words of the Human Rights Campaign's Evans, "rapid changes in custody and visitation case law." The *Lawrence* decision, she explains, "really helped us because for a long time, especially in adoption cases, judges restricted gay parents' rights on the grounds that sodomy was a felony." But now the baton has been passed to lawmakers, who know that courts are more deferential to legislators on questions of family policy than on issues of sexual privacy.

"Kids Need a Mom and Dad": Even Americans otherwise favorably disposed to gay rights may have concerns about how growing up in a gay household affects children. Traditionalists have done their best to heighten those concerns, arguing that discriminatory laws serve the best interests of kids.

The Phantom Menace

The mantra that "children need a mother and a father" has acquired a patina of conventional wisdom through frequent repetition. Yet there is little evidence that children raised by gay couples fare worse than other children.

Gay rights opponents such as Family Research Institute chief Paul Cameron and the Family Research Council's Timothy Dailey are fond of arguing that gay men are disproportionately likely to molest children—a potent charge rejected by the serious social scientists who have directly investigated it. Large-scale studies of molestation victims have repeatedly found that abusers overwhelmingly were either heterosexual in adult relationships or lacked any sexual response to adults.

Noting that about a third of molestation cases involve male adults targeting male children, Dailey and Cameron insist those adults must, by definition, be homosexual. Since homosexual men make up a far smaller proportion of the general population, Dailey reasons, gay men must be disproportionately likely to abuse children.

There is little evidence that children raised by gay couples fare worse than other children.

The problem with this view is that psychologists generally regard pedophilia an orientation of its own. Men who molest boys are not necessarily—indeed, are almost never—"gay" in the colloquial sense. Even if one accepts a definition that calls such men "homosexual," the fact remains that there is little overlap between that group and men who pursue romantic relationships with other adult men, the relevant comparison group for gay adoption.

Child Welfare Professionals' Opinions

Most child welfare professionals don't see things Dailey and Cameron's way. After reviewing the available data in 2002, the American Academy of Pediatrics endorsed second-parent adoption rights for gay couples. A resolution passed by the American Psychological Association in 2004 declared that there was "no scientific evidence that parenting effectiveness is related to parental sexual orientation: lesbian and gay parents are as likely as heterosexual parents to provide supportive and healthy environments for their children." It also noted that "the children of lesbian and gay parents are as likely as those of heterosexual parents to flourish."

The Child Welfare League of America, an organization founded in 1920 that now comprises more than 1,100 public and private agencies providing child services, filed an amicus [friend of the court] brief in 2004 supporting the ACLU's challenge to Florida's adoption ban, noting the consensus that "children are not adversely affected by their parents' lesbian or gay orientation" and that "all of the mainstream professional organizations in the fields of child health and welfare agree that there is no basis to exclude gay men and lesbians from adopting children." That same year, an Arkansas circuit court overturned a state Child Welfare Agency Review Board regulation prohibiting gay foster parenting after extensive fact finding, including testimony from a variety of psychologists, social workers, and sociologists, concluding that the ban contradicted the agency's mandate to serve the best interests of children.

The statistical evidence meshes with the experience of Adam Pertman, executive director of the Donaldson Institute, an adoption policy-research organization, and author of *Adop-*

tion Nation. "The evidence on the ground, based on the markers that we have, is that these are good families," he says. "The social workers I talk to are asking how they can recruit more [gay parents], because they're working. That's the best validation I can think of, unless you think all these child welfare professionals are out to harm kids."

Opponents of gay parenting, for the most part, have been forced to fall back on the assertion that the jury's still out. Noting—correctly—that none of the research on children of gay couples made use of the large random samples that generate the most robust results, they claim studies to date provide no basis for supposing that gay parents won't be inferior. But as New York University sociologist Judith Stacey argues, "they have to stretch pretty far to find that. The studies have been very consistent and very positive." Stacey concedes that most of them are "small scale" but adds that "there are some 50 studies now, and we don't see them going the other way. I have yet to see one legitimate refereed publication or scholar come out with a generally negative finding."

As in so many other disputes, child welfare may be serving as a proxy for a values debate. Marjorie Heins, director of the Free Expression Policy Project at the National Coalition Against Censorship and author of *Not in Front of the Children: "Indecency," Censorship, and the Innocence of Youth*, puts it this way: "If you're convinced that certain attitudes and values are wrong, then you consider exposing a child to those values a harm in itself."

Opponents of gay parenting ... have been forced to fall back on the assertion that the jury's still out.

The Second-Parent Trap

Even on the assumption that heterosexual households are somehow better for children, some restrictions on gay parenting are hard to fathom. For children in Florida's foster care system, the alternative to gay parents may be no parents at all. And many policies don't *prevent* gay couples from raising children; they just make life *more difficult* for gay parents and their children.

Barriers to second-parent adoption in some states create a variety of difficulties for gay couples raising children, often allowing only one to be recognized as a legal parent. Allison Bauer is an attorney who sits on the board of the Family Pride Coalition, an advocacy group for gay families. She lived in Virginia before moving to Massachusetts, where she could adopt her partner Marie Longo's biological children, twin girls. During the pregnancy, says Bauer, "we told our friends that if Marie went into labor, they should drive her into D.C. and *then* call an ambulance—we knew D.C. would issue an amended birth certificate with both our names later, and Virginia wouldn't." Until they moved, she adds, "I spent 14 months holding my breath. One night when the kids were six months old, Rebecca woke up with a terrible barking cough. We knew it was croup, and I had to wake Marie up because I was afraid the hospital would question my authority to authorize care, even though I had a document that gave me power of attorney."

Some restrictions on gay parenting are hard to fathom.

Such fears are why Anne Magro is fighting to overturn an Oklahoma law stipulating that "this state, any of its agencies, or any court of this state shall not recognize an adoption by more than one individual of the same sex from any other state or foreign jurisdiction." Magro, an accounting professor at the University of Oklahoma, had moved from New Jersey, where the state had granted her partner of 13 years, Heather Finstuen, second-parent rights over Magro's biological daughters.

Oklahoma state Rep. Thad Balkman (R-Norman), who supported the adoption law, defends it as a "reflection of our public policy that we support one-man-one-woman adoptions. To grant privileges like birth certificates to people who aren't in that relationship is doublespeak; we have to be consistent." Yet Balkman also claims that all the rights "so-called parents" have when their adoptions are recognized can be obtained through other means, such as by obtaining durable power of attorney for the second parent.

Brian Chase, an attorney with the gay rights litigation firm Lambda Legal who is representing Magro and Finstuen, disagrees. "A final adoption decree entitles a child to Social Security benefits and medical benefits that can't be conferred by a power of attorney," he says. "Furthermore, the most important right guaranteed by a final adoption is the right to continue to care for a child if something were to happen to the other parent. No power of attorney or will confers the degree of security that accompanies an adoption." And such workarounds, Magro adds, are often complex, time-consuming, and expensive.

Full Faith and Credit

New York University law professor Linda J. Silberman, an expert in interjurisdictional legal conflicts, believes policies like Oklahoma's may violate the Constitution's Full Faith and Credit Clause, which says "Full Faith and Credit shall be given in each State to the public Acts, Records, and judicial Proceedings of every other State." "If you're talking about one state applying another state's *law*," Silberman explains, "there's a public policy exception. If you have a court judgment from another state, though, you can't just say 'oh, we have a different public policy' and ignore it on that basis."

But the 1996 Defense of Marriage Act stipulates that "the United States Constitution shall not be construed to require any state or territory to give effect to any public act, record, or judicial proceeding respecting a relationship between persons of the same sex that is treated as a marriage under the laws of another state or territory." That attempt to reach judicial proceedings, normally not subject to "public policy exceptions," adds a new wrinkle, says Silberman. A state hostile to gay rights might, for instance, refuse to recognize a custody ruling from another state that allowed civil unions.

That scenario isn't just a hypothetical: It has already happened. In 2003 Lisa and Janet Miller-Jenkins, a lesbian couple who had been together since 1998 and were joined in a Vermont civil union in 2000, split up. Lisa moved to Virginia with her biological daughter and filed for dissolution of the union—and child support—in a Vermont court. Vermont awarded Janet visitation rights, as it might for a divorcing married couple. But when Virginia passed its Marriage Affirmation Act, which declared same-sex "civil unions . . . and any rights created thereby . . . void and unenforceable," Lisa appealed to Virginia to, in effect, declare that Janet was just a nice lady who once lived with Mommy. Frederick County Circuit Court Judge John Prosser did just that, and the case is now in the hands of the Virginia Court of Appeals. . . .

Family Values

At a breakout workshop on adoption, a few dozen participants studied the details of that choice. Panelists related their experiences adopting through private agencies, through foster care, and from the shrinking number of foreign countries open to gay parents. They recounted spending tens of thousands of dollars, waiting anxious months, sitting through lengthy and intrusive interviews and "home studies," and filling out mountains of paperwork in a process one likened to "buying a house and applying to grad school simultaneously. . . ."

Those behind the burgeoning assault on gay parenting would have us believe these people are a menace to the children they would take in.

Gay Men and Women Should Not Be Allowed To Adopt Children

Glenn T. Stanton

Glenn T. Stanton is the Director of Family Formation Studies at Focus on the Family, a national Christian organization that advocates for the family unit to remain intact. He is also the author of several books and co-author of Marriage on Trial: The Case Against Same-Sex Marriage and Parenting.

In Massachusetts, you won't find the words "husband" and "wife" on marriage applications. Clerks of the court performing marriages are instructed to use "party A" and "party B" instead. And it won't be long before we see "parent A" and "parent B," rather than "mother" and "father" on birth certificates and adoption records. The family is being made genderless.

But we must all ask if these changes in our understanding of family are harmless. The social sciences have a great deal to say about this, as we will see momentarily. But before we look at what they can tell us, we must start with what they cannot tell us.

"Don't Worry. The Kids Will Be Fine!"

Same-sex advocates are quick to assure us that children with same-sex parents are happy and healthy:

- "A growing body of scientific literature demonstrates that children who grow up with 1 or 2 gay or lesbian parents fare as well in emotional, cognitive, social, and sexual functioning as do children whose parents are heterosexual"[1]

- "Studies comparing groups of children raised by homosexual and by heterosexual parents find no developmental differences between the two groups of children. . . ."[2]

- "All the scientific evidence points to no differences among children raised in heterosexual or homosexual families."[3]

Do We *Know* They Will Be Fine?

But is it true? Research tells us no such thing, simply because there is no *reliable* body of research that compares children being raised in same-sex versus mother/father homes (this is still largely true in 2009). We are just beginning the same-sex family experiment; therefore there are not significant populations of such families for scientists to observe over long periods of time.

We are just beginning the same-sex family experiment.

Honest researchers confess as much:

- "Research exploring the diversity of parental relationships among gay and lesbian parents is just beginning."[4]

- "Thus far, *no work* has compared children's long-term achievement in education, occupation, income and other domains of life"[5] (emphasis added).

1. Ellen C. Perrin, MD, "Technical Report: Coparent and Second-Parent Adoption by Same-Sex Parents," *Pediatrics*, Vol. 109 No. 2, (2002) p. 341.
2. American Psychological Association, *APA Online*, www.apa.org/pubinfo/answers (15 August 2004).
3. Ed Susman, "AMA Backs Same-Sex Adoption," *Washington Times*, June 16, 2004; www.washingtontimes.com/upi-breaking/20040615-035749-1425r.htm (16 June 2004).
4. Perrin, 2002, p. 343.
5. Judith Stacey and Timothy Biblarz, "(How) Does the Sexual Orientation of Parents Matter?" *American Sociological Review*, 66 (2001), pp. 159–183.

- "From a sound methodological perspective, the results of these studies can be relied on for one purpose—to indicate that further research. . .is warranted. The only acceptable conclusion at this point is that the literature on this topic does not constitute a solid body of scientific evidence."[6]

- Studies on same-sex parenting are plagued with "persistent limitatation[s]. . . . As a result, we cannot be confident concerning the generalizability of many of the findings. . . ."[7]

- The authors of an *American Sociological Review* study, though personally sympathetic with the idea of the same-sex family, "disagree with those who claim that there are no differences between the children of heterosexual parents and children of lesbigay parents. . . ."[8]

It confirms that children do best when raised by their biological, married mothers and fathers.

What Research *Does* Tell Us

So that's what the research *doesn't* tell us. But what *does* solidly replicated research confirm? It confirms that children do best when raised by their own married mothers and fathers.

- "An extensive body of research tells us that children do best when they grow up with both biological parents. . . . Thus, it is not simply the presence of two

6. Affidavit of Steven L. Nock, *Halpern et al., v. The Attorney General of Canada*, Ontario Superior Court of Justice, March 2001, Court File No. 684/00, par. 130–131.
7. David Demo and Martha Cox, "Families with Young Children: A Review of Research in the 1990s," *Journal of Marriage and the Family*, 62 (2000), p. 889.
8. Judith Stacey and Timothy Biblarz, "(How) Does the Sexual Orientation of Parents Matter?" *American Sociological Review*, 66 (2001) 159–183.

parents, as some have assumed, but the presence of two biological parents that seems to support child development."[9]

- "Most researchers now agree that together these studies support the notion that, on average, children do best when raised by their two married, biological parents."[10]

- "Almost everyone—a few retrograde scholars excepted—agrees that children in mother-only homes suffer harmful consequences: the best studies show that these youngsters are more likely than those in [mother/father] families to be suspended from school, have emotional problems, become delinquent, suffer from abuse and take drugs."[11]

- "Overall, father love appears to be as heavily implicated as mother love in offsprings' psychological well-being and health."[12]

- "Female-headed households reported the greatest number of chronic [physical health] conditions for their children, regardless of racial or ethnic status."[13]

- Health scores are 20 to 35 percent higher for children living with both biological parents, compared with those living in single or stepfamilies.[14]

9. Kristin Anderson Moore et al., "Marriage From a Child's Perspective: How Does Family Structure Affect Children, and What Can We Do About It?" *Child Trends Research Brief*, June 2002, p. 1.
10. Mary Parke, "Are Married Parents Really Better for Children?" *Center for Law and Social Policy*, May 2003, p. 1.
11. Jame Q. Wilson, "Why We Don't Marry," *City Journal*, www.cityjournal.org/html/12_1_why_we.html. (20 October 2004).
12. Ronald P. Rohner and Robert A. Veneziano, "The Importance of Father Love: History and Contemporary Evidence," *Review of General Psychology* 5.4 (2001): 382–405.
13. Ronald J. Angel and Jacqueline Worobey, "Single Motherhood and Children's Health," *Journal of Health and Social Behavior* 29 (1988): 38–52; Ronald J. Angel and Jacqueline L. Angel, *Painful Inheritance: Health and the New Generation of Fatherless Families*, (Madison: University of Wisconsin Press, 1993).
14. Deborah A. Dawson, "Family Structure and Children's Health and Well-being: Data from the National Health Interview Survey on Child Health," *Journal of Marriage and the Family*, 53 (1991): 573–584.

- "When young boys have primary caretakers of both sexes, they are less likely as adults to engage in woman-devaluing activities and in self-aggrandizing, cruel or overly competitive male cults."[15]

- "We should disavow the notion that 'mommies can make good daddies,' just as we should disavow the popular notion of radical feminists that 'daddies can make good mommies.' . . .The two sexes are different to the core, and each is necessary—culturally and biologically—for the optimal development of a human being."[16]

So, we must ask, "Is it wise to enter the same-sex family experiment with a generation of children so we can learn how it will turn out?" Is it ethical to turn thousands of children into human guinea pigs simply because some adults desire such families? The answer must be a resounding "no."

This is especially true when we already have strong indicators that children who don't live with both a mother and father fare worse than those who do. Thanks to the sexual revolution in the 60s and 70s, with its baggage of no-fault divorce, unwed childrearing, stepfamilies, and fatherlessness, we have had ample opportunity to witness and record the results of fatherless and motherless childrearing.

Learning from the Divorce Experiment

We entered our national divorce experiment with all the best hopes, assuming that if parents could leave unhappy marriages, they would become happier parents, raising happier

---

15. Mary Stewart Van Leeuwen, *My Brother's Keeper: What the Social Sciences Do (and Don't) Tell Us About Masculinity*, (Downers Grove, IL: InterVarsity Press, 2002), p. 121. See also Scott Coltrane, "Father-Child Relationships and the Status of Women: A Cross-Cultural Study," *American Journal of Sociology* 93 (1988): 1085.
16. David Popenoe, *Life Without Father: Compelling New Evidence That Fatherhood and Marriage are Indispensable of the Good of Children and Society*, (New York: The Free Press, 1996), p. 197.

children. Advocates pushing the divorce experiment called forth a few authorities who assured us that children are resilient and they would adjust to living apart from their parents. "Love would see them through" we were told, much like same-sex family advocates seek to assure us today.

Well, the millions of children who were subjected to this experiment tell us a different story, as witnessed by multiple studies:

- The American Academy of Pediatrics, the same organization that tells us the same-sex family will work out just fine, now tells us that divorce "is a long, searing experience. . .characterized by painful los[s]es."[17]

- "Divorce is usually brutally painful to a child," and 25 percent of adult children of divorce continue to have "serious social, emotional, and psychological problems." Meanwhile, only 10 percent of adult children from intact families had such problems.[18]

- "Children in post-divorce families do not, on the whole, look happier, healthier, or more well-adjusted even if one or both parents are happier. National studies show that children from divorced and remarried families are more aggressive toward their parents and teachers. They experience more depression, have more learning difficulties, and suffer from more problems with peers than children from intact families. Children from divorced and remarried families are two to three times more likely to be referred for psychological help at school than their peers from intact families. More of them end up in mental health clinics and hospital settings."[19]

17. George J. Cohen, et al., "Helping Children and Families Deal With Divorce and Separation," *AAP Clinical Report*, 110 (2002): 1019–1023.
18. E. Mavis Hetherington, *For Better or For Worse: Divorce Reconsidered*, (W.W. Norton, 2002), p. 7.
19. Judith Wallerstein, *et al.*, *The Unexpected Legacy of Divorce: A 25 Year Landmark Study*, (Hyperion, 2000), p. xxiii.

Also, a convincing body of research shows us that children do not do as well when their mothers or fathers marry other people. And since it is biologically impossible for a child living in a same-sex home to be living with both natural parents, all same-sex homes are either literally step-families—formed after the end of a heterosexual relationship—or step-like, in that only one parent has a biological connection to the child.

The data on such families gives us great concern in forming more of them:

- "Social scientists used to believe that, for positive child outcomes, stepfamilies were preferable to single-parent families. Today, we are not so sure. Stepfamilies typically have an economic advantage, but some recent studies indicate that the children of stepfamilies have as many behavioral and emotional problems as the children of single-parent families, and possibly more. . . .

  Stepfamily problems, in short, may be so intractable that *the best strategy for dealing with them is to do everything possible to minimize their occurrence*"[20] (emphasis added).

- Children from stepfamilies, where the biological father is missing, are 80 times more likely to have to repeat a grade and twice as likely to be expelled or suspended, compared to children living with both biological parents.[21]

- Compared to their peers in biologically derived mother/father homes, children in stepfamilies endure significantly higher degrees of emotional and behavioral

20. David Popenoe, "The Evolution of Marriage and the Problems of Stepfamilies: A Biosocial Perspective," in Alan Booth and Judy Dunn, eds., *Stepfamilies: Who Benefits? Who Does Not?* (Hillsdale, N.J.: Lawrence Erlbaum Associates, 1994), p 5, 19.
21. Nicholas Zill, "Understanding Why Children in Stepfamilies Have More Learning and Behavior Problems Than Children in Nuclear Families," in Alan Booth and Judy Dunn, eds., *Stepfamilies: Who Benefits? Who Does Not?* (Hillsdale, N.J.: Lawrence Erlbaum Associates, 1994), p. 100.

problems, greater needs for psychological help and reports of poorer general health, along with increased likelihood of depression.[22]

Increased risks of physical and sexual child abuse at the hands of non-biological parents are another serious concern for same-sex families:

- Research on child-abuse indicates that preschool children who live with one biological parent and one stepparent are 40 times more likely to become a victim of abuse than children living with a biological mother and father.[23]

- Findings such as this led domestic violence researchers, Martin Daly and Margo Wilson, to conclude, "stepparenthood per se remains *the single most powerful risk factor* for child abuse that has yet been identified."[24]

- Compared to children in biological homes and even single-parent homes, "stepchildren are not merely 'disadvantaged,' but imperiled"[25] (emphasis added).

- Children residing in a home with a stepparent are eight times more likely to *die* of maltreatment than children living with two biological parents.[26]

- "Before the late 1970s, CSA [child sexual abuse] was regarded as rare. In the following decades, the incidence—based on official statistics—increased dramati-

22. Bonnie Barber and Janice Lyons, "Family Process and Adolescent Adjustment in Intact and Remarried Families," *Journal of Youth and Adolescence,*" 23 (1994): 421–436; Popenoe, 1994, p. 5.

23. Martin Daly and Margo Wilson, "Child Abuse and Other Risks of Not Living with Both Parents," *Ethology and Sociobiology,* 6 (1985): 197–210.

24. Martin Daly and Margo Wilson, *Homicide,* (New York: Aldine de Gruyter, 1988), p. 87–88.

25. Margo Wilson and Martin Daly, "Risk of Maltreatment of Children Living With Stepparents," in R. Gelles and J. Lancaster, eds., *Child Abuse and Neglect: Biosocial Dimensions,* (New York: Aldine de Gruyter, 1987), p. 230.

26. Michael Stiffman, *et al.,* "Household Composition and Risk of Fatal Child Maltreatment," *Pediatrics,* 109 (2002), 615–621.

cally." One of the major reasons for this increase was "the nature of the relationship between the child and perpetrator."[27]

More kids were living in homes with non-biological parents, therefore more kids were at risk for sexual abuse.

Increased risks of physical and sexual child abuse at the hands of non-biological parents are another serious concern for same-sex families.

Conclusion

A wise and compassionate society always comes to the aid of motherless or fatherless children, but a wise and compassionate society never intentionally creates motherless or fatherless families. But every single same-sex home would do exactly that, for no other reason than that a small handful of adults desire such kinds of families.

There is no research indicating such homes will be good for children. In fact the data show us that the family experimentation we have subjected children to over the past 30 years has *all* failed to improve child well-being in any important way. What makes us think more of it will make the situation any better? It will only make life for our children dramatically worse.

27. Frank Putnam, "Ten Year Research Update Review: Child Sexual Abuse," *Journal of the American Academy of Child and Adolescent Psychiatry* 42 (2003) 269-279.

Transgendered Persons Should Be Permitted To Have Custody of Children

Kari Carter

Kari Carter works for the law firm of Ulmer and Berne in Cleveland, Ohio.

Every day in the United States a judge determines whether it is in the best interests of a child to award custody to a divorcing mother or father. In applying this standard, courts consider a number of factors, including, *inter alia* [among other things], the physical, mental, emotional and social needs of the child; the parent's ability and desire to meet those needs; and the moral fitness of the parent. The breadth of the best interests of the child test allows judges wide discretion in their decision-making. This discretion allows a judge to consider factors that may negatively impact a child's life. However, courts have identified factors such as parent's race and religion as being outside the court's analysis; thus, considering them non-factors in child custody decisions.

Recently courts have addressed whether a parent's sexual orientation should be used when determining the custodial placement of a child. Case analysis reveals that the judicial system is currently split on how to treat a parent's sexual preference in relation to custody determinations; some courts only consider homosexuality if it negatively impacts the child, other courts view a gay parent as a per se ban on custody. Related to the confusion is the issue of how a court should treat a parent who identifies with the gender opposite to that which he was born. . . .

Kari Carter, "The Best Interest Test and Child Custody: Why Transgender Should Not Be a Factor in Custody Determinations," *Health Matrix: Journal of Law Medicine*, vol. 16, 2006, pp. 209–210, 214–224, 232–233. Copyright © 2006 Case Western Reserve University School of Law. Reproduced by permission.

The Best-Interests Standard

Child custody claims lie within state jurisdiction, and such disputes regularly appear in state and local courts. When addressing child custody claims, the court system makes a presumption that children, unlike adults, are unable to determine and safeguard their own interests. As a result, child placement laws are intended to ensure that children are provided an environment that sufficiently serves their needs. Child custody decisions are typically not reviewable and are not overturned unless the trial court commits gross and palpable error. Such an unpredictable decision setting provides extraordinary risks for a transgender parent.

In cases where the dissolving marriage consists of a natural and non-natural parent, many states make a presumption in favor of the natural parent. This presumption is made even when the non-natural parent has functioned as a parent. Non-natural parents seeking custody of a child must usually prove by a preponderance of the evidence that the natural parent is unfit. However, surrogacy and same-sex parent law indicate a shift in judicial thought, and courts are granting custody to non-natural parents who intended the birth of the child. . . .

The court will apply . . . the "best interest of the child" standard to determine the parental rights and responsibilities of each parent.

In the absence of a private child custody agreement, and sometimes even where there is an agreement, the courts will often intervene in child custody issues. In such situations the court will apply, with the intention of protecting the child's psychological and physical well-being, the "best interest of the child" (BIOC) standard to determine the parental rights and responsibilities of each parent. In determining what is in the best interests of the child, courts often employ court-appointed investigators and experts who interview the parents and children.

The Uniform Marriage and Divorce Act (UMDA), presented by the Commissioners on Uniform State Laws, provides the following factors as a guideline to determine the child's best interests:

(a) the wishes of the child's parent or parents as to his/her custody;

(b) the wishes of the child as to his/her custodian;

(c) the interaction and interrelationship of the child with his/her parent or parents, his/her siblings, and any other person who may significantly affect the child's best interest;

(d) the child's adjustment to his or her home, school, and community; and

(e) the mental and physical health of all individuals involved.

The court shall not consider conduct of a parent that does not affect his relationship to the child. All fifty states have included either portions or the entirety of the UMDA's BIOC standard in their statutes or through case law. However, there is a lack of consensus among legal, judicial, and mental health communities regarding a child's best interests, and courts have considerable discretion to make case-by-case decisions.

The BIOC standard is often criticized because the vast discretion provided to the judge allows bias to enter the judgment. Wide discretion and little oversight allow judges to use their individual subjective attitudes about parent behaviors and choices to resolve custody disputes. For instance, if a judge determines that factors such as a parent's religion, lifestyle preferences, gender, or race are important to a child's welfare, such factors may be used to determine a parent's custody award. In fact, a preference for a "traditional lifestyle" and the parent who can provide such a lifestyle is one of the main factors used to determine the best interests of the child. Typically, the inclusion of such factors in the application of the BIOC standard [according to the American Law Institute,] "usually reflect[s] prejudice rather than a rational assessment of the child's welfare."

A Definition of Transgender

In general, the transgender definition includes "transsexual people (who may or may not pursue medical treatments to change their bodies), cross-dressers, 'drag queens,' 'drag kings,' and men and women, regardless of sexual orientation, whose appearance or characteristics are perceived to be gender atypical." A person's identification of himself or herself as a male or female is their gender identity. Gender expression refers to how a person expresses their gender identity, through behavior, clothing, or appearance. Transgenders "include those who identify with the gender opposite their birth sex," [write Jason Cianciotto and Sean Cahill]. Female-to-male transgenders (FTM) are born with female bodies but identify with the male gender, whereas male-to-female transgenders (MTF) are born with male bodies but identify with the female gender.

A major debate surrounding the transgender definition is whether it includes only people who obtain sex reassignment surgery or hormones or whether such a definition includes men or women who identify themselves as the gender opposite that which they were born. The surgical procedure involved in a male-to-female sex-reassignment surgery includes removal of the penis, creation of an artificial vagina by turning the penis inside out, and rerouting of the urethra. The female-to-male sex-reassignment surgery involves a number of surgeries, including phalloplasty (construction of a penis), mastectomy, and hysterectomy. Due to the number of surgeries and resulting difficulties involved in the female-to-male

sex-reassignment surgery, many opt for a phalloscrotal pros-
thesis or an elongated clitoris, which results from taking
hormones. . . .

---

*Gender expression refers to how a person expresses their
gender identity, through behavior, clothing, or appearance.*

A debate residing in the medical profession is whether
transgenderism is a mental disorder. The DSM IV-TR [*Diagnostic and Statistical Manual of Mental Disorders*, Fourth Edition, text revised] classifies a "transgendered or transsexual"
person as having a psychiatric disorder, given the name gender
identity disorder (GID). However, there are no known biological or medical reasons or social causes for the disorder.

Transgender Parents and Child Custody

The path to a child custody issue involving a transgender involves a number of legal steps, all of which are not consis-
tently treated in state legislatures or courts. Most states have
yet to decide what makes someone "legally" a male or a female. Transgenders can enter a marriage in one of two ways:
(1) they can be in a legal, heterosexual marriage prior to their
gender identity change or (2) they can identify themselves as a
transgender and subsequently enter a marriage. Regardless of
the beginnings, a transgender marital relationship can involve
children either through a biological tie with one parent, assisted reproductive technologies, adoption, or surrogacy.

Unfortunately, statistics show that many transgender marriages end in divorce. Historically, transgender marriage disso-
lutions have resulted in either complete denial of the transgendered parent's custody and visitation with the children or
supervised visitation rights for the transgendered parent.

Some courts have shown blatant prejudice towards transgenders in denying child custody. In *In re Darnell*, a mother's

parental rights were terminated because of her continuing relationship with her former husband, a male-to-female transsexual, whose parental rights had already been terminated. In its opinion the court cited a case holding that parental rights may be terminated when the custodial parent does not leave an abusive partner. However, the case at hand presented no evidence that the transgender parent was abusive.

Most states have yet to decide what makes someone "legally" a male or a female.

A number of social science arguments have been used to prevent a transgender person from obtaining custody of a child with whom they have developed a parental relationship. Courts have allowed testimony that a child's understanding about sexuality might be negatively affected by continued contact with the transgender parent. Courts have also entertained the idea that a child's mental and emotional health will be affected by trouble in understanding the transgender parent's transition, the disturbance to their relationship with their transgender parent, and conflicts in the relationship between their parents. In *Cisek v. Cisek*, an Ohio Appeals Court denied visitation rights to a father who decided to undergo sex reassignment after the divorce. In support of its decision, the court cited medical testimony that the children might experience mental harm and difficulty in adjusting their relationship with their father. In *J.L.S. v. D.K.S.*, the court reversed an order of joint custody after the father pursued gender reassignment surgery. The court refused any visitation until "the children . . . [were] emotionally and mentally suited for physical contact with their father. . . ."

There is also a fear that a child's peer relationships may be adversely affected through the stigma attached to the transgender parent. In *Daly v. Daly*, the Nevada Supreme Court, over a strong dissent, upheld the termination of a natural father's parental rights after he underwent sex reassignment surgery. The court's decision was based on the effect his identity had on his daughter. Evidence was provided that his ten-year-old daughter was extremely upset by her father becoming a woman, telling the court that she did not want to visit him. In a parting shot, the court asserted that "[i]t was strictly Tim Daly's choice to discard his fatherhood. . . ." Upon review of this case, [transgender rights activist] John M. Ohle stated that although a child may not be able to accept their parent's transgender way of life and will most likely receive some social prejudice on behalf of the transgender parent, "never have courts ruled that a social animus is sufficient justification to terminate parental rights."

Some courts have granted transgender parents custody and visitation rights upon the condition that the transgender repress their gender identity issues and keep them secret from the children. In *In re Marriage of D.F.D. and D.G.D.*, a father who had cross-dressed, but who was in therapy and whose child was unaware of the cross-dressing, won a reversal of a trial court decision granting sole custody to the mother and only supervised visitation to the father.

Although courts have typically viewed a transgender parent as a threat to a child's best interests, some courts have found a transgender [person] as a parent to be non-threatening. In *In re Custody of T.J.*, an appeals court affirmed the decision to award child custody to a male-to-female transgender. The court reasoned its decision by citing the child's knowledge of and ability to deal with his father's transgender identity. The court stated that there was no evidence that the child had any gender identity confusion of his own and there was no evidence that the transgender parent would provide future issues for the child. Similarly, in *Christian v. Randall*, the court denied a father's attempt to regain custody from a former wife who had become a male because the children were happy and well-adjusted. In making its decision, the court relied on a Colorado statute that precludes the court's consideration of "conduct . . . that does not affect [the parent's] relationship with the child."

The little data that exist show that children of transgender parents are not negatively impacted by their parent's gender dysphoria.

Scientific Evidence

There are no available statistics regarding how many children in the United States have a transgender parent. However, recent statistics estimate that up to one-third of the transgenders attending a gender identity clinic have children. The amount of published research examining the social and psychological development of children of transgender parents is astoundingly small. However, the little data that exist show that children of transgender parents are not negatively impacted by their parent's gender dysphoria.

In 1978, a study was conducted regarding the sexual identity of thirty-seven children raised by homosexual or transsexual parents. The children ranged in age from three to twenty years and lived in the sexually atypical households for one to sixteen years. Thirty-six of the children report or recall childhood toys, games, clothing, and peer group preferences that are typical for their sex. The thirteen older children who reported erotic fantasies or overt sexual behaviors were all heterosexually oriented. The same author of the 1978 study published a similar study in 1998, which concluded that children of transgender parents are "more likely to be hurt by a traumatic separation from their parent than because of that parent's gender identity."

A separate investigation was conducted in the United Kingdom in 2002 to examine whether and how parental gender role influences children's gender development, mental health, family relationship and peer relationships. The data collected from the investigation repeated the conclusion of the 1978 study and reported that none of the children developed any characteristics of their own gender identity disorder. . . .

The definition of family in the United States is a changing concept.

The authors of the 2002 report also report similarities between the feelings of loss and disruption of a child of a transgender parent and those of children experiencing other familial losses or disruptions, such as the separation of parents, a new partner of a parent, or the prolonged illness or medical treatment of a parent. Both the 1978 study and the 2002 report suggest that children of transgender parents are likely to experience difficulties in the familial relationship. However, nothing in either study indicates that these difficulties are much different from other, similar difficulties that children of non-transgender parents experience while growing up. . . .

The Changing Family

The definition of family in the United States is a changing concept, and a number of family situations exist where non-parents play the parental role in a child's life. Although not currently given priority within the legal system, non-parents have shown that they are capable of raising children in environments that are just as caring and functional as those found in the traditional family. In fact, the American Law Institute's Principles of Law of Family Dissolution has recognized two new categories of parents that address the evolving family: "parent[s] by estoppel" and "de facto" parents. A "parent by estoppel" has "lived with the child since the child's birth, holding out and accepting full and permanent responsibilities as parent, as part of a prior co-parenting agreement with the child's legal parent. . . ." A "de facto" parent has resided with the child and, with the consent of the legal parent, performed a share of parental functions.

Regardless of their gender identity, a transgender [person] can be a natural parent or fill the role of either a parent by estoppel or a de facto parent. Therefore, even though the law may not legally recognize a transgender as a parent, biology and familial roles will provide the transgender an opportunity to fill such a role. Thus, whether or not the law wants to legally award child custody to transgenders, family constructs involving transgenders in parental roles will exist.

In situations where a transgender plays the role of a parent, either biologically or socially, the individual is afforded the opportunity to function as a "good parent," the same opportunity given to any parent. As discussed above, state legislatures have used the BIOC standard to describe the characteristics that afford one parent preferred custodial status. Generally, the BIOC standard seeks to evaluate the abilities of a parent to provide for the physical, mental, and emotional needs of the child. Therefore, whichever parent is able to provide the most in relation to the child's needs should be awarded custody of the child.

Adoption or Long-Term Placement with Relatives Is Better than Foster Care

Mark Testa, Nancy Sidote Salyers, Mike Shaver, and Jennifer Miller

Mark Testa and Judge Nancy Sidote Salyers are Co-Directors of Fostering Results. *Mike Shaver is Deputy Director of* Fostering Results, *and Jennifer Miller is Senior Associate at Cornerstone Consulting Group.* Fostering Results *is a national, nonpartisan public-education project to raise awareness of issues facing children in foster care.*

The past decade has seen unparalleled success in finding adoptive homes for children in foster care. This achievement—including states' answering the federal challenge to double adoptions out of foster care in five years—was the result of coordinated efforts across multiple fronts. At the national level, the Adoption and Safe Families Act (ASFA) of 1997 required that states pursue adoptive homes for children who had been in foster care for 15 out of the latest 22 months. Federal policy also linked adoption performance to financial rewards by offering bonuses to states increasing the numbers of adopted foster children. State agencies and courts rallied to the call by setting goals, tracking timelines, and expediting legal processes to secure the placement of foster children in safe and permanent homes.

Despite the noteworthy accomplishments, serious work remains for the estimated 185,700 foster children still awaiting permanence. The importance of finding these children safe and permanent homes is a federal and state priority. But a

Mark Testa, Nancy Sidote Salyers, Mike Shaver, and Jennifer Miller, "Family Ties: Supporting Permanence for Children in Safe and Stable Foster Care With Relatives and Other Caregivers," Urbana, IL: Fostering Results, Children and Family Research Center, October, 2004, pp. 1–4, 6, 9. Reproduced by permission.

long-recognized permanency option that ASFA reaffirms is under-utilized by states working to secure permanence for children—especially those children in safe and stable placements with relative caregivers. This permanency option is legal guardianship, and the focus of this report is how children in long-term foster care with relatives are prime candidates for permanence when supported through some form of subsidized guardianship.

Forty-six thousand children—one out of every four of the 185,700 awaiting permanence in long-term foster care in the United States—live in relative foster care. Research supports this practice. Studies show that children cared for by kin are safer and less likely to change living arrangements than children in unrelated foster care. Even with the benefits, retaining children in safe kinship foster care placements does not provide children a permanent legal home, and it does not come without significant administrative costs. When the state retains legal custody, the government—through a caseworker and a judge—is the only legally recognized decision-maker for the child. Tasks like routine immunizations, school pictures, and out-of-state trips can require prior approval and multiple signatures. Relatives raising children in foster care are subject to routine court appearances, quarterly case reviews and monthly visits by caseworkers which limit the privacy that other families take for granted. A caseworker can decide at any time to remove the child from the relative's home. While these activities serve an important purpose when the child welfare system is engaged in preparing a child to return to his or her parents or ensuring the safety of a foster care placement, these same activities can be an unnecessary burden for relative caregivers, especially once a judge has decided that reunification with biological parents is not an option. In such cases, the better choice is for government to get out of the lives of these families by converting safe and stable kinship foster placements into legally permanent homes. Unfortunately, the lack of financial assistance for an additional permanency option—like subsidized guardianship—is creating barriers to these conversions. States receive federal resources to help provide adoption assistance to relative families. However, under current law, states do not receive federal child welfare resources for guardianships (with the exception of a limited number of states discussed later in this report that have received "waivers" of federal financing rules to provide guardianship assistance).

By supporting legal guardianship with a subsidy the same way federal policy now supports adoption, additional children in long-term foster care with kin could join the thousands of children who have already left the child welfare system for adoptive homes. Subsidizing legal guardianship complements subsidized adoption and builds on the strengths that foster care by grandparents, aunts, uncles and other relatives brings when children can no longer be looked after by their birth parents and a court determines that adoption is not an appropriate option for them. Using recently released 2002 federal AFCARS [Adoption and Foster Care Analysis and Reporting System, U.S. Department of Health and Human Services] data, there are an estimated 19,250 children in long-term care with relatives where a court has determined that they cannot be safely returned to their parents and has also determined that adoption is not an option. Subsidized guardianship gives states an important tool for moving these 19,250 children out of long-term foster care and into safe, loving, and permanent homes once reunification and adoption have been ruled out.

Studies show that children cared for by kin are safer and less likely to change living arrangements than children in unrelated foster care.

The fact that there is no federally funded assistance program supporting children discharged from foster care to the legal guardianship of relatives limits the ability of states to replicate the successes of other states in reducing the number of foster children in long-term placements with kin. Subsidized guardianship is increasingly emerging as an important policy solution at both federal and state levels. States continue to pursue the prospect of funding guardianship with federal dollars through the waiver process, and legislation to create a federally funded subsidized guardianship program has been introduced in Congress. The research makes a strong case that federal reimbursement facilitates permanence and assists in ending the legal uncertainty of relative foster care by bringing stability and security to the thousands of foster children who are—by any measure—already home.

Assisting Families

The federal Adoption and Safe Families Act of 1997 recognizes both adoption and guardianship as viable legal alternatives for pursuing permanence for children in kinship foster care when reunification is not possible. Adoption transfers all rights and duties from birth parents to adoptive parents. It works well for relatives who have raised the children from birth, don't know the parents' whereabouts, or know them to be a continuing safety threat to the children. Legal guardianship also transfers these same rights and duties, but it allows birth parents to maintain a presence in their children's lives. Unlike adoption, guardianship does not require terminating parental rights and recasting extended family relations into the nuclear family mould of parent and child. It works well when relatives prefer to retain their extended family identities as grandparent, aunt or uncle instead of becoming mom or dad. It also serves as a viable alternative when there are insufficient grounds to terminate parental rights, or children object to having their ties legally severed from their biological parents and siblings. For example, a biological parent dealing with profound physical or mental disabilities may not be able to care for her child, yet the best interests of the child may not be well-served by forcing a termination of parental rights. In such circumstances, subsidized guardianship offers a way for relatives to step in while still retaining the family bond. With the option of subsidized guardianship, families and judges have the flexibility to lend legal permanence to existing family bonds in a way that best respects cultural norms and strengthens the role of extended family.

While both adoption and guardianship are technically recognized in federal statute, federal financing laws effectively limit guardianship as a permanency choice by continuing federal financial assistance only to relatives who remain foster parents or adopt. Under existing federal financial regulations, relative foster parents who become legal guardians are not eligible for federally supported child welfare assistance if they assume permanent legal guardianship for the child. While states can and do financially support guardianships in some jurisdictions, there exists a clear financial disincentive to move a child from a placement where the cost is shared by the federal government (foster care) to a placement supported solely by state dollars. In effect, the absence of a federally supported guardianship program not only limits an important permanency option for thousands of families incapable of supporting the entire cost of care on their own, the continuing availability of federal payments for relatives as long as they continue to provide care to an open child welfare case inflates the number of children in more costly public foster care.

An estimated 46,000 children in kinship foster care in the United States have been under the legal responsibility of the state for longer than 17 out of the most recent 22 months. Interestingly, if these same children were in unrelated foster family or group care, federal law would direct states to file a petition terminating the rights of their parents and approve a qualified family for an adoption. While federal law directs states to file a petition terminating the rights of children who have been in care for 17 months, the state may choose to exempt individual children living with relatives from this requirement.

Children in safe and stable relative foster care are, for all practical purposes, already living with family.

This exclusion wisely recognizes that children in safe and stable relative foster care are, for all practical purposes, already living with family. In many of these cases, the termination of parental rights would only serve to disrupt the nuclear bond that legally ties extended kin to the child. The unfortunate consequence of this exemption for relatives is that it gives states the erroneous impression that they no longer have any affirmative obligation to pursue permanence for many of these 46,000 children—77% of whom have been living in the same relative home for a year or more and 27% for four years or more. It can be argued that most of these children are already safely home. The continuation of child welfare agency and court oversight of these families adds cost and unnecessary governmental intrusion.

In the late 1990s, several states responded to the federal invitation for child welfare demonstrations by applying for waivers to test the feasibility of extending financial assistance to foster parents willing to become the legal guardians of the children under their care when reunification and adoption have been ruled out. The aim of these federal and state waiver demonstrations was to determine whether offering guardianship subsidies to families could boost the rate of permanence for children in foster care above levels observed for families not offered guardianship as an option. Because waiver demonstrations test new approaches in policy and financing, they have the benefit of being constructed using what's known as an experimental design. Using an experimental design ensures that randomly constructed control and demonstration groups are similar enough to verify whether or not the added option of subsidized guardianship as a permanency choice actually improves permanency rates (reunification, adoption and guardianship combined) for those families given the choice.

Since 1997, a total of seven states (Delaware, Illinois, Maryland, Montana, New Mexico, North Carolina and Oregon) have implemented federal waivers to provide subsidies to relatives who become the legal guardian of children in the custody of the child welfare agency—a practice currently not supported within existing federal guidelines that govern reimbursable costs to the states (Title IV-E of the Social Security Act). In Montana and New Mexico, children under the jurisdiction of the Tribal courts were included in the demonstration project. All of the states with IV-E waivers provide a monthly guardianship subsidy that is equal to or less than the current foster care payment, with approximately half of the cost borne by the federal government. Generally, subsidies in these states were offered to relatives and foster parents who have been caring for the children for at least one year and for whom reunification and adoption by the prospective guardian have been ruled out as permanency options. . . .

The continuation of child welfare agency and court oversight of these families adds cost and unnecessary government intrusion.

Fulfilling the Promise of Permanence

With the passage of ASFA, there was clear recognition of the importance of timely permanence for children placed in foster care. It also sought to support the unique and important role that relatives can play in the lives of children who can no longer live with their parents. While both are important goals, taken together the result for children placed with relatives has been a slow move to permanence. The large number of children living with relatives who have remained in foster care more than two years highlights a missed opportunity for the nation's child welfare system. These placements—the safest and most stable for children in care—are commitments recognized in policy, but not now financially supported in practice.

The lessons learned from innovative efforts in various child welfare jurisdictions point to subsidized guardianship as an additional pathway to permanence for this group of children. The evidence is clear: supporting legal guardianship from foster care the same way IV-E supports adoptions promotes the goal of permanence for children. Moreover, in most cases, these placements can be supported at less cost to taxpayers because there is a reduction in the administrative costs associated with managing and overseeing an open foster care case. The evidence also suggests that how the program is funded makes a difference. Those subsidized guardianship programs that relied exclusively on state dollars made uneven progress in converting stable relative placements into permanent homes, while federal support through waivers helped states promote subsidized guardianship as a permanency option for relative caregivers.

While securing better outcomes at less cost is an independently compelling rationale, the real justification for making subsidized guardianship available lies in the benefits for children and those families who have stepped up to care for them. Even the best functioning bureaucracies struggle to minimize the impact that serving an open child welfare case can have on family life. The intrusions that ongoing agency and judicial oversight impose on families may make sense as long as the time away from home is temporary and the plan for the children is reunification with parents. But once reunification is no longer an option and adoption is ruled out and safety has been assured, subsidized guardianship offers a cost-effective and proven alternative to retaining these children in state custody.

Grandmothers Who Raise Their Grandchildren Experience More Stress

Terry L. Mills, Zenata Gomez-Smith, and Jessica M. De Leon

Terry L. Mills is an associate professor of psychology at the University of Florida. Zenata Gomez-Smith is a doctoral student in criminal justice and law at the University of Florida. Jessica M. De Leon is coordinator for Research Program Services at the University of Florida College of Pharmacy.

U.S. Census reports indicate that nearly 5.5 million children under age 18 co-reside in homes with a grandparent. This number represents about 7.7% of all children under age 18 in the United States. Further, about 1.3 million of these children live in grandparent-headed households where neither parent is present; and roughly half of the grandchildren in such families are under age 6.

It is not a new phenomenon for a grandparent to intervene or assist in raising their grandchildren or other relatives. Rather, what is new is the dramatic increase in this phenomenon. For example, [census researchers Ken] Bryson and [Lynne] Casper reported that between 1992 and 1997, the greatest growth in intergenerational co-residence occurred among grandchildren living with grandparents with no parent present. [Sociologists Catherine Chase] Goodman and [Merril] Silverstein reported that although most grandparent-headed households provide for the grandchild and one or both parents, approximately 36% have neither parent living in the home, implying that the grandparents have complete responsibility for the care of the grandchild.

Terry L. Mills, Zenata Gomez-Smith, and Jessica M. De Leon, "Skipped Generation Families: Sources of Psychological Distress Among Grandmothers of Grandchildren Who Live in Homes Where Neither Parent Is Present," *Marriage and Family Review*, vol. 37, no. 1/2, April 19, 2005, pp. 192–193, 197–198, 206–210. Copyright © 2005 Haworth Press. Reproduced by permission of Taylor & Francis Group, LLC, http://www.taylorandfrancis.com.

[Gerontologists Esme] Fuller-Thompson, [Meredith] Minkler, and [Diane] Driver have referred to grandparent-headed households where neither parent is present as, "skipped generation" families. These skipped generation families have increased as a consequence of several social problems including: the increase in drug abuse, teen pregnancy, divorce and the rapid rise of single-parent households, mental and physical illness, AIDS, crime, child abuse and neglect, and incarceration of parents. The increase in the number of grandchildren and grandparents who co-reside reflects sociodemographic characteristics of the grandparents and their progeny, as well as contemporary social problems.

The purpose of this study was to examine skipped generation households to determine the context wherein grandmother caregivers of grandchildren experience psychosocial distress. Specifically, the study was concerned with the effects of the sociodemographic characteristics of the grandmother and grandchild, factors associated with the grandmother's social support, the grandchild's physical health and access to health care; and the grandmother's perceived parental burden. An advantage of this study is that the data are from a national probability sample, which allows us to make inferences about the U.S. population. . . .

These skipped generation families have increased as a consequence of several social problems.

The Study

Much of the previous research on the psychological well-being of caregiving grandparents have been comparative studies that examined the sources of stress of non-caregiving grandparents versus caregiving grandparents; or caregiving grandparents versus parents. Moreover, these prior studies have primarily emphasized the effect on psychological distress of the grand-

parent re-entering the parental role, the grandparent's perception of caregiver burden, the grandparent's health status, or
the quality of the relationship with the parents. However,
there is a dearth of empirical studies that have explicitly conducted within-group analyses of the factors associated with
psychosocial distress among grandmothers in skipped generation households. For example, little is known about how the
demographic or health/behavioral factors of the grandchild
are related to the skipped generation grandmother's psychosocial distress. Additionally, there are not many studies that have
investigated whether the variance in the frequency of psychosocial distress among skipped generation grandmothers is associated with their own demographic characteristics, or the
context of their social support. Finally, only a few previous
studies of grandparent caregivers have employed national
probability samples. Based upon a review of the relevant literature and our interest in expanding our understanding of
the factors associated with the psychosocial distress of grandmothers in skipped generation households, we investigated the
following research questions:

1. Does the grandchild's race, sex, or age influence the
   grandmother's frequency of feeling psychosocial distress?
2. Does the grandmother's race, sex, or age, affect the frequency of feelings of psychosocial distress?
3. What factors associated with the grandmother's social
   support are related to the frequency of psychosocial distress?
4. In what ways does the grandchild's physical health and
   access to health care influence the occurrence of the
   grandmother's psychosocial distress?

The data for the present study are from the 1999 wave of
the National Survey of America's Families [NSAF] that is designed to produce estimates that are representative of the ci-
vilian, noninstitutionalized population under age 65. In order

to reduce respondent burden, a decision was made to sub-sample household members. If there were multiple children under age 6, one was randomly selected (Focal child #1). The same was done for children ages 6 to 17 (Focal child #2). No more than two children were sampled from each household. Data were collected about each of these sample children through the most knowledgeable adult (MKA) in the household for that child. In choosing the MKA, interviewers asked to speak to the person in the household who knew the most about the sampled child's education and health care. In families with two sampled children, the MKA was not necessarily the same person for both children. Consequently, there were cases in which one family had two MKAs.

The NSAF draws households from two separate sampling frames. The first frame consists of households from a random-digit dial (RDD) sample of households with telephones. However, because households without telephone service contain a disproportionate number of low-income children, a supplementary area sample was conducted in person for those households without telephones. The area sample provides data for these and other families without current phone service. . . .

Often, grandparent caregivers neglect their own physical and emotional health because they give priority to the needs of their grandchildren.

Oversize samples were drawn in 13 states (Alabama, California, Colorado, Florida, Massachusetts, Michigan, Minnesota, Mississippi, New Jersey, New York, Texas, Washington, and Wisconsin) to allow the production of reliable estimates at the state level. Further, the oversize state samples were supplemented with a balance of the U.S. sample to allow the creation of estimates at the national level as well.

Grandparents and Stress

Grandparent caregivers face a myriad of challenges in nearly all aspects of their lives when they assume the role of parent. As a result, they are prone to psychological and emotional strain as well as feelings of helplessness and isolation. Often, grandparent caregivers neglect their own physical and emotional health because they give priority to the needs of their grandchildren. It has been argued that grandparent caregiving is largely a "women's issue" and that this gendered perspective can be viewed from a broader sociological context of caregiving vis-à-vis the ambivalent accounts of grandmothers raising their grandchildren as "silent saviors," while also being disparaged for their perceived failures as parents of their own children. Moreover, as a "women's issue" grandparent caregiving is a social problem that largely affects low-income women.

The present study examined grandmother caregivers in skipped generation households to determine the ways that social factors such as gender, age, race, the context of the grandmother's social support, and the grandchild's health status or access to health care affect the frequency of psychosocial distress of grandmothers in skipped generation households. Several important associations emerged from our analyses.

When we accounted for the effects of the grandmother's and the grandchild's demographic characteristics we found that younger grandmothers were likely to experience psychosocial distress more frequently than their older counterparts. This finding is consistent with prior studies reporting that younger grandparents experienced higher levels of anxiety and psychological stress. It has been suggested that younger grandparents are highly likely to experience psychological stress in trying to adjust to the demands of their own careers and personal interests. However, in our study, the negative effect of being a younger grandparent was negated when we controlled for the effects of the grandmother's social support mechanisms. This suggests the importance of social assistance especially for younger grandmother caregivers, to help them to fulfill their own lives, while coping with the responsibilities of providing care for their grandchildren, in the absence of biological parents from the household.

Our finding that married grandmothers reported feeling psychosocial distress less frequently than their non-married counterparts is consistent with previous studies reporting that individuals who are married or have a partner report lower rates of depressive symptoms, relative to those without a partner. The positive effect of being married or having a partner may be partially explained by the adaptation process and family stress theory. Although we did not have a measure of relationship quality, and the data did not allow us to examine whether or to what extent the husbands and partners provided caregiving assistance to the grandmothers, adaptation strategies and efforts to minimize the stress of providing care for the grandchildren are plausible explanations; and we presume that the positive benefits of marriage/partnering found in our study can be attributed to the help and support received by the grandmothers from their mates. Of course, it is not marriage per se, but the quality of the relationship that can strongly affect a person's emotional well-being. A related finding was the positive effect of having other relatives living in the household. Similar to the positive benefits of having a spouse or partner, having relatives living in the household may likely contribute to the successful adaptation of the family, and contribute to the caregiving and support of the grandchild.

Younger grandparents experienced higher levels of anxiety and psychological stress.

It is no surprise that not receiving welfare payments for childcare, or having a family income below the poverty level (e.g., severely poor or near poor) were associated with more frequent feelings of emotional distress. One serious consequence of becoming a custodial grandparent is a change for the worse in the grandparent's financial status. Previous investigations have shown that the majority of custodial grandparents reported having less money than before they assumed custody; and that their current incomes were inadequate to meet their grandchildren's needs. One reasonable explanation for the positive effect of not receiving welfare is that under the present welfare structure Temporary Assistance for Needy Families (TANF) has work requirements, time limits, and other restrictions that may be difficult to manage for many grandmother caregivers. These requirements may constrain a low-income grandparent's ability to receive benefits for her family, and thus exacerbate an already difficult economic situation.

Our findings indicated that almost 68% of the grandmothers had family incomes in the severely poor to near poor range. Minkler points out the historic differences in the level of aid afforded widowed mothers versus mothers who were single as a result of non-marriage, divorce, or desertion, and later between foster care and Aid to Families with Dependent Children. She notes the controversy over whether grandmothers are more "deserving" of aid than single mothers, or foster parents, for that matter. The welfare reform of 1996 continues this historical inequity and selectivity and fuels the controversy over who is deserving of public assistance. Many grandparent caregivers from low-income families encounter difficulties in obtaining public assistance and making ends meet. For example, Temporary Assistance for Needy Families (TANF) funds cannot be used to provide assistance to a family that includes an adult who has received such assistance for 60 months. Any previous use as first-generation parents counts against the caregiving grandparent by restricting the duration of their eligibility for public assistance. Furthermore, the majority of grandchildren of younger caregiving grandparents are most likely co-residing with their grandchildren for three or more years and a considerable number do so for five or more years. A grandmother might want to work rather than receive welfare, but for those without a husband or partner who could provide childcare or work more himself, increasing her hours of work is difficult.

It is interesting that grandparents who reported having a usual place for health care also reported more emotional distress. Intuitively, we might have anticipated that having a usual place for health care would facilitate better care for the grandchild, thus, less emotional distress. However, although somewhat speculative, a plausible explanation is that this finding might be due to the stress of having to interact more frequently with a health care system that does nothing to eliminate the complexity or make it easier for caregiving grandparents to obtain health care for their grandchild. For example, grandparents may need legal authority to get their grandchildren medical care, and to enable them to receive immunizations and vaccinations, public assistance, and supportive services. Also, as pointed out by [Margaret E.] Weigers and colleagues, many "usual care" providers do not have office hours that are convenient, or are often difficult to contact. More research into this aspect of the context social support of skipped generation households is warranted. Qualitative research would be especially useful in understanding the meaning of, and satisfaction with access to health care for this population of grandparent caregivers.

One serious consequence of becoming a custodial grandparent is a change for the worse in the grandparent's financial status.

In considering the importance of regional differences in the context of skipped generation households, . . . several questions [arise] for future research. For example, in the Midwest, why do the "women's issues" (e.g., being poor and female; or being Black and female) produce such disparate outcomes? For example, overall, what is it about living in the Midwest compared to other regions of the United States that diminishes the negative effect of poverty on psychosocial distress for skipped generation grandmothers? One answer might be that the comparatively small proportion of poor people, less stressful lifestyle, and less debasing access to public support make being poor more tenable, compared to other regions of the country. Yet, for Black grandmothers living in the Midwest, these same positive socioenvironmental factors produce strikingly opposite outcomes. It is reasonable to consider that in part, among Black skipped generation grandmothers living in the Midwest the greater frequency of feeling psychosocial distress might be attributed to social isolation, alienation, and the loss of important life roles, such as "traditional" (non-custodial) grandparenting, leisure pursuits, and free time. Unfortunately, from these data, there is no way to test this proposed theory. Therefore, it is imperative that researchers conduct national qualitative studies looking at the subjective meaning of being a skipped generation grandparent with an eye towards uncovering regional distinctions. . . .

It is apparent that more favorable consideration must be given to public assistance for caregiving grandparents especially to poor women who are more likely to be the caregivers in skipped generation households. It is imperative that more policy makers acknowledge the social good accomplished by these women caregivers, who are struggling to keep their families intact, despite incredible barriers. An exemption from the welfare-related time limit is a starting point to assisting the skipped generation grandparents, who, for the most part, are truly disadvantaged.

Organizations to Contact

The editors have compiled the following list of organizations concerned with the issues debated in this book. The descriptions are derived from materials provided by the organizations. All have publications or information available for interested readers. The list was compiled on the date of publication of the present volume; the information provided here may change. Be aware that many organizations take several weeks or longer to respond to inquiries, so allow as much time as possible.

Abolish Adoption
PO Box 401, Palm Desert, CA   92261
e-mail: info@abolishadoption.com
Web site: www.abolishadoption.com

Abolish Adoption is an organization that petitions to end the practice of adoption. Abolish Adoption lobbies, protests, petitions, and sues for open birth and adoption records. Its publications include *The Ultimate Search Book: Worldwide Adoption, Genealogy and Other Search Secrets* by Lori Carangelo.

Alternative Family Matters
PO Box 390618, Cambridge, MA   02139
(617) 576-6788
e-mail: jenifer@alternativefamilies.org
Web site: www.alternativefamilies.org

Alternative Family Matters is an agency that assists lesbians, gay men, bisexuals, and transgendered people (LGBTs) who want to have children through adoption, artificial insemination, or surrogacy. The agency also educates the medical community to better understand and serve LGBT-headed families. Alternative Family Matters created the Conception Connection Registry and Counseling Service, which specializes in facilitating parenting arrangements between otherwise unrelated men and women who want to have children together.

American Adoption Congress (AAC)

PO Box 42730, Washington, DC 20015
(202) 483-3399
Web site: www.americanadoptioncongress.org

The AAC is an educational network that promotes openness and honesty in adoption. It advocates adoption reform, including open adoption records. The AAC publishes the quarterly *Decree* and has position statements available on its Web site.

Bastard Nation

PO Box 1469, Edmond, OK 73083-1469
(415) 704-3166
e-mail: bn@bastards.org
Web site: www.bastards.org

Bastard Nation advocates for the civil and human rights of adult citizens who were adopted as children. The organization campaigns for the access of birth and adoption records. Bastard Nation's publications include *The Basic Bastard*, a book of articles on adoptee rights, and the *Bastard Quarterly* newsletter.

Child Welfare Information Gateway

1250 Maryland Ave. SW, 8th Floor, Washington, DC 20024
(800) 394-3366
e-mail: info@childwelfare.gov
Web site: www.childwelfare.gov

The Child Welfare Information Gateway is a service of the Children's Bureau in the Administration for Children and Families, part of the U.S. Department of Health and Human Services. The Child Welfare Information Gateway promotes the safety, permanency, and well-being of children and families by connecting child welfare, adoption, and related professionals to essential information. Resources available at the Web site include the National Foster Care & Adoption Directory.

Child Welfare League of America (CWLA)
2345 Crystal Drive, Suite 250, Arlington, VA 22202
(703) 412-2400 • fax: (703) 412-2401
Web site: www.cwla.org

The CWLA, the nation's oldest and largest membership-based child welfare organization, has been known and respected as a champion for children since 1920. The primary objective of CWLA, and the title of both its current strategic plan and its National Framework for Community Action, is *Making Children a National Priority*. The CWLA engages all Americans in promoting the well-being of children and young people and protecting them from harm. Its publications include *Children's Voice*, a magazine, and the bimonthly journal *Child Welfare*.

Children's Rights Council (CRC)
8181 Professional Place, Suite 240, Landover, MD 20785
(301) 459-1220
e-mail: info@crckids.org
Web site: http://crckids.org

The CRC works to ensure a child the frequent, meaningful, and continuing contact with two parents and extended family that the child would normally have if his or her parents were married. CRC works to strengthen families through education, favoring family formation and family preservation. Unlike many other organizations with some of the same concerns, CRC is genderless; it is neither a women's group nor a men's group. Rather, it advocates what it believes to be the best interests of children, including the Children's Bill of Rights.

Concerned United Birthparents (CUB)
PO Box 503475, San Diego, CA 92150-3475
(800) 822-2777 • fax: (858) 712-3317
e-mail: info@cubirthparents.org
Web site: www.cubirthparents.org

Concerned United Birthparents is a nonprofit organization providing support for family members separated by adoption. CUB has support groups for birth parents and seeks to educate the public about the lifelong impact on all who are touched by adoption. CUB publishes a newsletter, *CUB Communicator*, and has available on its Web site the booklet *What You Should KNOW If You're Considering Adoption for Your Baby.*

Dave Thomas Foundation for Adoption

4150 Tuller Road, Suite 204, Dublin, OH   43017
(800) 275-3832
e-mail: info@davethomasfoundation.org
Web site: www.davethomasfoundation.org

The Dave Thomas Foundation for Adoption is a nonprofit public charity dedicated to dramatically increasing the adoptions of the more than 150,000 children waiting in North America's foster care systems. Created by Wendy's founder Dave Thomas, who was adopted as a child, the foundation works to fulfill its mission by implementing result-driven national signature programs, awareness initiatives, and advocacy efforts. As the only foundation dedicated exclusively to foster care adoption, the foundation is driven by Dave's simple value: Do what's best for the child. The foundation's brochure, *A Child Is Waiting: A Step by Step Guide to Adoption*, answers general questions about adoption and the foster care adoption process.

Evan B. Donaldson Adoption Institute

120 E. Thirty-eighth Street, New York, NY   10016
(212) 925-4089
e-mail: info@adoptioninstitute.org
Web site: www.adoptioninstitute.org

The Evan B. Donaldson Adoption Institute provides leadership that improves adoption laws, policies, and practices through sound research, education, and advocacy to better the lives of everyone touched by adoption. To achieve its goals, the institute conducts research, offers education to inform public opinion, promotes ethical practices and legal reforms, and works to translate policy into education. The institute issues a monthly e-newsletter on its Web site and has published numerous white papers, policy briefs, and policy perspectives, including *Adoption by Lesbians and Gays: A National Survey of Adoption Agency Policies, Practices, and Attitudes; Expanding Resources for Children: Is Adoption by Gays and Lesbians Part of the Answer for Boys and Girls Who Need Homes?* and *Expanding Resources for Waiting Children II: Eliminating Legal and Practice Barriers to Gay and Lesbian Adoption from Foster Care.*

Families for Private Adoption (FPA)
PO Box 6375, Washington, DC   20015-0375
(202) 722-0338
e-mail: info@ffpa.org
Web site: www.ffpa.org

FPA is an adoption support and education group that advocates and encourages private (nonagency) adoptions. FPA hosts educational programs for couples seeking to adopt. The group publishes a newsletter and a guide to successful adoption, the *Adoption Book.*

The Fatherhood Coalition
PO Box 310, Turners Falls, MA   01376
(617) 723-DADS
Web site: www.fatherhoodcoalition.org

The Fatherhood Coalition advocates for the institution of fatherhood, encompassing the full range of human behaviors and endeavors that flow from the father-child relationship. The coalition works to promote shared parenting and to end the discrimination and persecution faced by divorced and unwed fathers. Founded in 1993, the coalition strives to secure equal parenting rights and responsibilities for men and women by raising awareness of the social problems and harm to children caused by fatherlessness, reversing government laws and policies that promote fatherlessness, restoring constitutional protections for fundamental rights in family law, and restricting state intrusions into the sanctity of the family.

Human Rights Campaign (HRC)
1640 Rhode Island Ave. NW, Washington, DC   20036-3278
(202) 628-4160 • fax: (202) 347-5323
e-mail: webmaster@hrc.org
Web site: www.hrc.org

HRC, America's largest civil rights organization working to achieve gay, lesbian, bisexual, and transgender (GLBT) equality, seeks to improve the lives of GLBT Americans by advocating for equal rights and benefits in the workplace, ensuring families are treated equally under the law, and increasing public support through innovative advocacy, education, and outreach programs. HRC works to secure equal rights for GLBT individuals and families at federal and state levels by lobbying elected officials, mobilizing grassroots supporters, educating Americans, investing strategically to elect fair-minded officials, and partnering with other GLBT organizations.

Institute for Adoption Information (IAI)
409 Dewey Street, Bennington, VT   05201
(802) 442-2845
e-mail: info@adoptioninformationinstitute.org
Web site: www.adoptioninformationinstitute.org

IAI is a nonprofit organization of adoptees, birth parents, adoptive parents, adoption professionals, and others who have united to enhance the understanding of adoption. The institute advocates for balanced, accurate coverage of adoption in news and entertainment media. The IAI's publications include the brochure *Why It Is Important to Understand Adoption.*

National Adoption Center (NAC)
1500 Walnut Street, Suite 701, Philadelphia, PA   19102
(800) TO-ADOPT
Web site: www.adopt.org

Since 1972, when the National Adoption Center started, it has found families for more than twenty thousand children up for adoption. The National Adoption Center expands adoption opportunities for children living in foster care throughout the United States and is a resource to families and to agencies who seek the permanency of caring homes for children. The center offers an online family preparation training program—*The Adoption Roadmap*—for prospective adoptive and foster parents.

National American Council on Adoptable Children (NACAC)
970 Raymond Ave., Suite 106, St. Paul, MN   55114
(651) 644-3036 • fax: (651) 644-9848
e-mail: info@nacac.org
Web site: www.nacac.org

The NACAC promotes and supports permanent families for children and youth in the United States and Canada who are in foster care and who have special needs. The NACAC provides education and advocacy for adoption and offers leadership training to parents to help create and enhance support groups. The NACAC publishes a quarterly newsletter, *Adoptalk*.

Bibliography

Books

Thomas C. Atwood — *Adoption Factbook IV: The Most Comprehensive Source for Adoption Statistics Nationwide*. Washington, DC: National Council for Adoption, 2007.

Laura Beauvais-Godwin and Raymond Godwin — *The Complete Adoption Book: Everything You Need to Know to Adopt a Child*. Avon, MA: Adams Media, 2005.

Laura Christianson — *The Adoption Decision: 15 Things You Want to Know Before Adopting*. New York: Harvest House, 2007.

James L. Dickerson and Mardi Allen — *The Basics of Adoption: A Guide for Building Families in the U.S. and Canada*. Westport, CT: Praeger, 2006.

Martha J. Henry and Daniel Pollack — *Adoption in the United States: A Reference for Families, Professionals, and Students*. Chicago: Lyceum Books, 2009.

Sara Holloway, ed. — *Family Wanted: Adoption Stories*. London: Granta, 2005.

Kathleen Hushion, Susan B. Sherman, and Diana Siskind, eds. — *Understanding Adoption: Clinical Work with Adults, Children, and Parents*. Lanham, MD: Aronson, 2006.

Pamela Kruger and Jill Smolowe, eds.	*A Love Like No Other: Stories from Adoptive Parents.* New York: Riverhead Books, 2005.
Anne Lanchon	*Adoption: How to Deal with the Questions of Your Past.* New York: Harry N. Abrams, 2006.
Todd Parr	*We Belong Together: A Book About Adoption and Families.* New York: Little, Brown, 2007.
Jagannath Pati, ed.	*Adoption: Global Perspectives and Ethical Issues.* New Delhi: Concept, 2007.
Corrie Lynne Player	*The Everything Parent's Guide to Raising Your Adopted Child.* Avon, MA: Adams Media, 2008.
Pamela Anne Quiroz	*Adoption in a Color-Blind Society.* Lanham, MD: Rowman and Littlefield, 2007.
Jayne E. Schooler	*The Whole Life Adoption Book: Realistic Advice for Building a Healthy Adoptive Family.* Colorado Springs: NavPress, 2008.
Suzanne Buckingham Slade	*Adopted: The Ultimate Teen Guide.* Lanham, MD: Scarecrow Press, 2007.
Joanne Wolf Small	*The Adoption Mystique.* Bloomington, IN: 1stBooks, 2004.
Katarina Wegar, ed.	*Adoptive Families in a Diverse Society.* New Brunswick, NJ: Rutgers University Press, 2006.

Debra Shiveley Welch	*Son of My Soul: The Adoption of Christopher*. Carmangay, AB, Canada: Saga Books, 2007.

Periodicals

Kasi K. Addison and Nicole Marie Richardson	"Black Adoptions on the Rise," *Black Enterprise*, November 2005.
Gloria Batiste-Roberts	"Should Black Children Only be Adopted by Black Parents? Yes, They Must Be Taught Coping Techniques to Deal with Racist Practices," *Ebony*, September 2008.
Ellen Charles	"Where Do Babies Come From?" *Mother Jones*, November/December 2007.
Ross Douthat and Marshall Poe	"Adoption Options," *Atlantic*, September 2005.
Peggy Drexler	"No Such Thing as an 'Average' Family," *Newsweek*, May 14, 2007.
Merle Fletcher	"Talking About Adoption to Your Adopted Child," *Community Care*, July 10, 2008.
Christina Frank	"International Adoption," *Working Mother*, May 2007.
Ivy George	"Can Buy Me Love?" *Sojourners Magazine*, June 2006.

Liza P. Grey   "Working Toward Motherhood,"
                      Chronicle of Higher Education,
                      February 17, 2006.

Anita Hamilton   "When Foster Teens Find a Home,"
                      Time, June 5, 2006.

Malak Hamwi   "Sending Babies Abroad," *Newsweek*,
                      November 13, 2006.

Susanna   "A Baby Dream—Come True,"
Heckman   *Health*, March 2008.

Alexandra N.   "The 'Motherless' Child: Some Issues
Helper   in Adoption," *Psychiatric Times*,
                      February 2005.

Maggie Jones   "Looking for Their Children's Birth
                      Mothers," *New York Times Magazine*,
                      October 28, 2007.

Carl Koestner   "Family Secrets," *Commonweal*, April
                      20, 2007.

New Statesman   "Parenthood by Piggyback," October
                      23, 2006.

Emily Nussbaum   "The Nuclear Family, Exploded," *New
                      York*, August 20, 2007.

Anne-Marie   "Why Are American Babies Being
O'Neill, Joanne   Adopted Abroad?" *People*, June 6,
Fowler, and Ron   2005.
Arias

Katrina Onstad   "Bursting the Chinese Baby Bubble,"
                      Maclean's, May 19, 2008.

Felicia Persaud   "I Want to Adopt an Orphan from
                    Overseas," *New York Amsterdam
                    News*, February 15, 2007.

Meredith Resnick   "We Didn't Need the Past—or So I
                    Thought," *Newsweek*, July 3, 2006.

Tracey   "The Joy of Adoption," *Ebony*,
Robinson-English   November 2005.

Thom Rock   "Baby Boy #3331," *Yankee*,
                    March/April 2007.

Amanda Ruggeri   "A Quiet Fight over Gay Adoption,"
                    U.S. News & World Report, November
                    3, 2008.

Shelley Sperry   "The Politics of Adoption," *National
                    Geographic*, January 2008.

Tamra Thomas   "A Mother's Hope," *Good
                    Housekeeping*, December 2007.

Barbara Turvett   "A Great Way to Make a Family,"
                    Working Mother, November 2006.

Alison Stein   "A New Approach to Adoption,"
Wellner   *Chronicle of Philanthropy*, May 26,
                    2005.

Rosemary Zibart   "Teens Wanted," *Time*, April 4, 2005.

Index

A

Abandoned children
    "one-child" policy, China, 84,
      85, 91
    orphanages and, 49, 50, 86
    parental rights of, 22
    poverty and, 15, 73
Abortion issues, 49, 87, 117–118
Acquired immune deficiency syn-
    drome (AIDS), 74, 134
"Adoptable" children, 47
Adoptee issues
    best interest decisions, 82
    disabilities, 52
    displacement feelings, 62–63
    identity problems, 77–78,
      118–119, 123
    mutual consent registries,
      119–121
    unwanted contact, 115–115
Adoption agency issues
    abandonment disclosure, 91
    background checks, 28
    costs, 43–44, 45
    "donations" to, 88–89
    government regulation, 50–51,
      81
    Hague Convention, 18, 56–60
    lack of regard, 20–21
    private vs. public, 80
    registries, 94–95
    restrictions, 63
    scams, 39–40
    unwilling adoptions, 31–37
    U.S. vs. China, 88–89

Adoption and Foster Care Analysis
    and Reporting System
    (AFCARS), 167
Adoption and Safe Families Act
    (ASFA), 165, 168
Adoption "facilitators," 28–29, 40
Adoption in the United States
    (Henry, Pollack), 134–135
Adoption Nation (Pertman), 141–
    142
Adoption Promotion Act, 79
Adoption Under One Roof
    (website), 94
Adoptive parent issues
    counseling, 104
    emotional consequences,
      38–39
    mandatory openness, 115
    older potential parents, 67–73
    special needs children, 134–
      135
    unwilling adoptions, 31–37
    See also Open adoption issues
African adoptions
    community efforts and, 82–83
    identity issues with, 76–78
    orphan crisis and, 74–75
    resistance to, 81
    slavery effects, 75–76
    U.S. foster care and, 78–81
African American grandparent
    guardians, 181
Aid to Families with Dependent
    Children, 179
Allen, Faith, 42–43, 45–46
Allen, Lee, 41

American Academy of Pediatrics, 141, 151

American Civil Liberties Union (ACLU), 137

American Coalition for Fathers and Children, 23

American Psychological Association, 141

Andrew, Anita M., 84–92

Anti-father bias, legal system, 23

Asia Society, 90

Association of Asian American Studies, 90

Association of Asian Studies, 90

Association of Social Workers (NASW), 76–77

Atkins, Chris, 62–63

Atwood, Thomas C., 111–121

Axness, Marcy, 101–110

B

Baby buying, 33–35, 43, 51

"Baby Jessica," 101–103

"Baby Richard," 101

Babytrafficking rings, 85, 87

Balkman, Thad, 144

Bartholet, Elizabeth, 15, 50, 63

Baur, Allison, 143

Behreandt, Denise L., 56–60

Bell, Teri, 135

Best interest of the child (BIOC), 156–158, 164

Birth father issues

mandatory open records, 113–114

registries, 94–95, 119–121

regulation, 20–23

unwanted contact, 115–115

See also Contact issues

Birth mother issues

abortion, 117–118

changing minds, 62

in China, 85

counseling, 103–104

mandatory open records, 113–114

paid expenses, 45

privacy rights, 94

registries, 119–121

resentment, 130–132

unwanted contact, 115–115

See also Contact issues; Open adoption issues

Boirski, Leonette, 58–59

Bush, George W. (administration), 56, 87

C

Cambodian adoptions, 27, 40, 85

Cameron, Paul, 140

Canadian adoptions, 46

Carter, Kari J., 155–164

Casper, Lynne, 173

Caughman, Susan, 97–98

Celebrity adoptions, 14–15

Chase, Brian, 144

Child custody issues

birth father rights, 20–23, 96

gay parents' rights, 136–137, 139, 145

grandparent guardians, 179

legal guardianship, 171–172

open adoption, 101–110

by state, 166

transgender adoptions, 159–162

Child welfare assistance, 169, 178–179

Child Welfare League of America, 141

Children, Youth and Families Department (CYFD), 21

China Center for Adoption Affairs (CCAA), 50–51

Chinese adoptions
    as big business, 88–89
    concern for children, 53–55
    disclosure needed, 90–92
    guidelines for, 18–19, 87–88
    homosexual adoption ban, 48, 51–52
    impact on U.S. adoptions, 51–53
    international laws for, 47–49
    "one-child" policy, 49, 84, 87
    orphan classification in, 86
    as sender-country, 49–51

Christian v. Randall, 161–162

Cisek v. Cisek, 160

Clinton, Bill, 30

Closed vs. open adoptions, 101–110, 122–124

Contact issues, adoptive vs. birth families
    heartache, 122–132
    privacy rights, 111–121
    registries, 94–95
    See also Birth father issues; Birth mother issues; Mandatory open records; Open adoption issues

"Contact veto," 115–116

Convention on the Rights of the Child (CRC), 64, 77

Corruption issues
    in China, 54, 84–92
    fraud/scams, 27, 38–39, 40
    international adoptions, 24–30
    Vietnamese, 24–30, 85

    See also Hague Convention on Intercountry Adoption

Cote, John, 95

Council of Accreditation (COA), 59

Counseling issues
    adoptee's emotions, 123
    adoption attitudes, 108–109
    adoption costs, 44
    adoptive parents, 105–106
    client privacy, 112
    open adoptions, 103–104
    open records laws, 112
    See also Emotional issues

Crawford, Christina, 15

Crowley, Michael, 38–41

D

Dailer, Moriah, 96–100

Dailey, Timothy, 140

Daly v. Daly, 160–161

In re Darnell, 159–160

De Leon, Jessica M., 173–181

DeBoer/Schmidt adoption tragedy, 101–103

Defense of Marriage Act, 144–145

Department of Children and Families, 28–29

Dewey, Arthur E., 87

D.F.D. and D.G.D., In re Marriage of, 161

Disabilities in adoptees, 52

Divorce and gay adoptions, 150–154

D.K.S., J.L.S. v., 160

Domestic adoption rates, 79–80

Donaldson, Evan B., 43–44

Driver, Diane, 174

DSM IV-TR (Diagnostic and Statistical Manual of Mental Disorders), 159

E

Emotional issues
    adoption stress, 177–181
    grandparent guardians, 174–176
    open adoptions, 105–106, 108–110
    resentment, 130–132
    transgender parenting, 162–163
    transracial adoptees, 77–78
    See also Counseling issues; Identity issues
Ethica (regulation agency), 35
"Ethical adoptions," 39
Ethiopian adoptions, 81

F

Families with Children from China (FCC), 90
Family Pride Coalition, 143
Family relatives vs. foster care, 165–172
Family Research Council, 140
Family Research Institute, 140
Father registries, 22–23
Feinberg, Richard, 29
Female infanticide, 32
Female-to-male transgenders (FTM), 158–159
Focus on Children (adoption agency), 40
Foster care system (U.S.)
    adjustment problems after, 134

Hague Convention and, 57
international adoptions and, 62–63
mandatory openness and, 118
vs. permanency option, 165–168
"waiting" children, 78–81
    See also Gay and lesbian adoptions
Fraud/scam issues, 27, 38–39, 40
French adoptions, 46
Fuller-Thompson, Esme, 174

G

Galindo, Lauryn, 40
Gay and lesbian adoptions
    barriers to, 137–140
    China's ban on, 48, 51–52
    concerns over, 145–148
    divorce and, 150–154
    evidence supporting, 141–142
    family values and, 145
    molestation fears, 140–141
    vs. reproductive technology, 53
    research and, 148–150
    state bans of, 136–137, 142–144
    See also Transgender parenting
Gender identity disorder (GID), 159
Goldman, Russell, 31–37
Gomez-Smith, Zenata, 173–181
Goodman, Catherine Chase, 173
Grandparents as guardians
    emotional wellbeing of, 174–176
    stress on, 177–181
Greene, Melissa Fay, 14
Gritter, Jim, 104–105

Guatemala Adoptive Families Network, 58
Guatemalan adoptions, 29, 56, 57

H

Hague Convention on Intercountry Adoption (HCICA)
 adherence issues, 64–66
 child protection and, 18, 30
 in-country placement priority, 77
 kidnapping protection by, 32–33
 regulation issues of, 18, 56–60
 restrictions with, 57–58
Healthcare issues, 180
Hedstrom, Tedi, 26–27
Heins, Marjorie, 142
Henry, Matha, 134–135
Hoffman, Bruce and Debbie, 28
Homosexual adoptions. *See* Gay and lesbian adoptions; Transgender parenting
Howells, Dion, 106
Huddleston, Mark, 20–23
Human Rights Campaign, 137

I

Identity issues
 with African adoptions, 76–78
 closed adoptions, 123
 mandatory openness, 118–119
Immigration and Nationality Act (INA), 86
In-country adoption issues, 77, 82
India adoptions, 31–37, 44
International Adoption Association (Dublin), 44

International adoptions
 African orphans, 74–83
 Cambodian adoptions, 27, 40, 85
 Canadian adoptions, 46
 care options with, 65
 corruption issues with, 24–30
 Ethiopian adoptions, 81
 French adoptions, 46
 Guatemalan adoptions, 29, 56, 57
 India adoptions, 31–37, 44
 Ireland adoptions, 44–46
 Mexican adoptions, 46
 older potential parents and, 67–73
 Phillippine adoptions, 44
 regulations with, 45–46
 Romanian adoptions, 53
 Russian adoptions, 44, 69
 Thailand adoptions, 44
 Vietnamese adoptions, 24–30, 85
 after WWI, 14
 See also African adoptions; Chinese adoptions; Hague Convention on Intercountry Adoption
International Confederation of the Red Cross, 66
Ireland adoptions, 44–46

J

J.L.S. v. D.K.S., 160
Joint vs. single parenting, 148–150

K

Keane, Kerry, 97–100
Kidnapping protection, 32–33
Klima, Bill and Debra, 39–30

L

Latrace, Mai-Ly, 24–29
Lavin, Judith, 134
Lawrence v. Texas, 139
Legal guardianship issues
    open adoption, 168–171
    permanence, 171–172
    subsidizing, 165–168
    "waiver demonstrations," 170–171
Lesbian adoptions. *See* Gay and lesbian adoptions

M

Madonna (singer) adoptions, 14, 15
Magro, Anne, 143–144
Male-to-female transgenders (MTF), 158, 160
Mandatory open records
    adoptive parent and, 115
    birthparents' rights and, 113–114
    foster care concerns, 118
    medical information, 119
    unplanned pregnancies and, 116–118
    unwanted contact and, 114–115
    See also Open adoption issues
Marriage Affirmation Act, 145
Marriage issues
    adoption regulations, 48–49
    divorce "experiment," 150–154
    gay adoptions, 139
    grandparents as guardians, 178
Maskew, Trish, 25
McArthur, David and Dorrie, 124–132

McElroy, Wendy, 20–23
Medical information issues, 119
Mexican adoptions, 46
Miliband, David, 43
Miller, Jennifer, 165–172
Miller-Jenkins, Lisa and Janet, 145
Mills, Terry L., 173–181
Minkler, Meredith, 174, 179
Molestation issues, 140–141
Mommy Dearest (Crawford), 15
Money laundering, 27
Moore, Roy, 137, 139
Most knowledgeable adult (MKA), 176
Multiethnic Placement Act, 78–79
Muslim regulations, 81
Mutual consent registries, 119–121

N

National Association of Black Social Workers (NABSW), 76
National Center for Health Statistics, 94
National Center on Family Homelessness, 62
National Council for Adoption (NCFA), 39, 41, 111, 119–121
National Survey of America's Families (NSAF), 175–176
Natural disaster separations, 66
Nazario, Sonia, 122–132
"Non-Hague countries," 57–58
Non-natural parents, 156–157
Nongovernmental organizations (NGOs), 66
Nontraditional adoptions
    gay men and lesbians, 136–145, 146–154
    grandparents and, 173–181

relatives vs. foster care, 165–172

special needs children, 134–135

transgendered persons, 155–164

Not in Front of the Children: "Indecency," Censorship, and the Innocence of Youth (Heins), 142

O

Older potential parents
choosing children, 69–70
meeting children, 70–71
researching adoption, 68–69
taking children home, 71–73
"One-child" policy, China, 49, 84, 87

Open adoption issues
attitudes about, 108–110
closed adoptions, 101–110, 122–124
contact issues, 106–108
counseling, 103–104, 108–109
emotional consequences, 105–106, 122–132
family closeness, 96–100
fear/misunderstandings, 102–105
legal guardianship, 168–171
See also Mandatory open records

Orphan/orphanage issues
abandoned children, 49, 50, 86
African crisis, 74–75
"bribes," 88
Chinese classification, 86

P

Palmer, Caitriona, 42–46
Parental issues
abandoned children, 22
gay parents' rights, 136–137, 139, 145
in Hague Convention, 64–65
joint vs. single parenting, 148–150
mutual consent registry, 119–121
non-natural parents, 156–157
step-families, 152–153
See also Adoptive parent issues; Birth father issues; Birth mother issues; Grandparents as guardians; Marriage issues; Older potential parents

Paternity testing, 21
Pertman, Adam, 35, 141–142
Philippine adoptions, 44
Pickett, Rachel, 135
Pollack, Daniel, 134–135
Poncz, Elisa, 47–55
Pool, Kendall, 124–132
Poverty issues
abandoned children, 15, 73
child welfare, 178–179
grandparent guardians, 181
in international adoptions, 14, 35
orphans and, 74
The Primal Wound (Verrier), 107
Principles of Law of Family Dissolution, 163
Privacy rights, 111–121
Pruden, Marie, 67–73
Ptasnik, David, 59
Putative-father registries, 94

R

Racial awareness, 75–76
Radis, David, 16
Ramaswamy, Gita, 36
Ramirez, Belinda, 38–39
Randall, Christian v., 161–162
Registries, 94–95, 119–121
Regulation issues
    with birth fathers, 20–23
    in China, 47–55
    corruption, 24–30
    deception and, 38–41
    Hague Convention, 18, 56–60
    unwilling adoptions, 31–37
    U.S. success with, 42–46
Religious issues, 81, 157
Removal of Barriers to Interethnic
    Adoption Act, 79
Reproductive technology alternative, 53
Reunion advocacy, 112
Ritter, Andy, 29–30
Roane, Kit R., 24–30
Roby, Jini L., 74–83
Romanian adoptions, 53
Russian adoptions, 44, 69

S

Salyers, Nancy Sidote, 165–172
Same-sex family "experiment,"
    148–150
Sanchez, Julian, 136–145
Save the Children Alliance, 66
Scams. *See* Fraud/scam issues
Second-parent adoption. *See* Gay
    and lesbian adoptions
Sexual child abuse, 153–154
Shaver, Mike, 165–172
Shaw, Stacey A., 74–83

Silberman, Linda J., 144–145
Silverstein, Merril, 173
Single vs. joint parenting, 148–150
Skipped generation households.
    See Grandparents as guardians
Slavery effects, 75–76
Smolin, David and Desiree, 31–37
Special Kids Need Special Parents
    (Lavin), 134
Special needs children, 134–135
Spry, Mike, 106
Stacey, Judith, 142
Stanton, Glenn T., 146–154
State bans of gay adoptions, 136–
    137, 142–144
Step-families, 152–153
The Story of David (Howells), 106

T

Talton, Robert, 137
Temple, Bob and Alette Coble-
    Temple, 41
Temporary Assistance for Needy
    Families (TANF), 179
Testa, Mark, 165–172
Texas, Lawrence v., 139
Thailand adoptions, 44
Thatcher, Liane, 97–100
There Is No Me Without You
    (Greene), 14
T.J., In re Custody of, 161
Transgender parenting
    best-interests standard, 156–
    158, 164
    child custody and, 159–162
    court determinations on, 155
    definition of, 158–159, 163–
    164
    emotional issues, 162–163

See also Gay and lesbian adoptions
Transracial adoptions, 77–78

U

Uniform Marriage and Divorce Act (UMDA), 157
United Kingdon (U.K.), 44–45, 162
United Nations Children's Fund (UNICEF), 64–66, 74, 82
United Nations High Commissioner for Refugees (UNHCR), 66
United States (U.S.)
    adoption regulations in, 42–46, 88–89
    birthmother complications, 62
    China impact on, 51–53
    foster care system, 78–81
    welfare system, 45

Unplanned pregnancies, 116–118
Unwanted contact, 115–115
Unwilling adoptions, 32–36

V

Valois, Laura and Anthony, 38–39
Verrier, Nancy, 107
Vietnamese adoptions, 24–30, 85
Visa fraud, 27, 40

W

"Waiver demonstrations," 170–171
War-related separations, 66
Weigand, Camren, 96–100
Weigers, Margaret E., 180
Welcome House (adoption agency), 58–59
West, Carrie, 24–25, 27–28
Winerip, Michael, 96–100
World War I (WWI) adoptions, 14